ROME

ROME

DAY ONE

Andrea Carandini

Translated by Stephen Sartarelli

PRINCETON UNIVERSITY PRESS   PRINCETON AND OXFORD

First published in Italian under the title *Roma: Il Primo Giorno*
by Gius. Laterza & Figli S.p.A., Rome, in 2007

Copyright © 2011 by Princeton University Press

Requests for permission to reproduce material from this work should be sent to Permissions,
Princeton University Press

Published by Princeton University Press, 41 William Street, Princeton, New Jersey 08540

In the United Kingdom: Princeton University Press, 6 Oxford Street,
Woodstock, Oxfordshire OX20 1TW

press.princeton.edu

Library of Congress Cataloging-in-Publication Data

Carandini, Andrea.
[Roma. English]
Rome : day one / Andrea Carandini ; translated by Stephen Sartarelli.
p.   cm.
"First published in Italian under the title Roma: Il Primo Giorno by Gius. Laterza & Figli S.p.A.,
Rome, in 2007"—T.p. verso.
Includes bibliographical references and index.
ISBN 978-0-691-13922-7 (hardcover : alk. paper)
1. Rome—History—Kings, 753-510 BC. 2. Romulus, King of Rome. 3. Archaeology and history—
Italy—Rome. 4. Excavations (Archaeology)—Italy—Rome. 5. Mythology, Roman. I. Title.
DG233.3.C37513 2011
937´.6301—dc22   2010040559

British Library Cataloging-in-Publication Data is available

The translation of this work has been funded by SEPS
Segretariato Europeo per le Pubblicazioni Scientifiche

S·E·P·S

EUROPEAN SECRETARIAT FOR SCIENTIFIC PUBLICATIONS

Via Val d'Aposa 7, 40123 Bologna, Italy. seps@seps.it, www.seps.it

This book has been composed in Sabon

Printed on acid-free paper. ∞

Printed in the United States of America

10 9 8 7 6 5 4 3 2 1

Contents

———✦———

THE ORDERING OF THE REGNUM, OR THE *CONSTITUTIO ROMULI*

ROME

INTRODUCTION

—————

First Thoughts

Historians tell us that the oldest Rome was the *Roma Qua-drata*, a fenced settlement on the Palatine. . . . [W]e will ask ourselves how much a visitor . . . may still find left of these early stages in the Rome of today. . . . Of the buildings which once occupied this ancient area he will find nothing, or only scanty remains. . . . Their place is now taken by ruins, but not by ruins of themselves but of later restorations made after fires or destruction. . . . Now let us, by a flight of the imagination, suppose that Rome is not a human habitation but a psychical entity with a similarly long and copious past—an entity, that is to say, in which nothing that has once come into existence will have passed away and all the earlier phases of development continue to exist alongside the latest one. This would mean that in Rome the palaces of the Caesars and the Septizonium of Septimius Severus would still be rising to their old height on the Palatine, and the castle of S. Angelo would still be carrying on its battlements the beautiful statues which graced it until the siege by the Goths, and so on. But more than this. In the place occupied by the Palazzo Caffarelli would once more stand—without the Palazzo having to be removed—the Temple of Jupiter Capitolinus; and this not only in its latest shape, as the Romans of the Empire saw it, but also in its earliest one, when it still showed Etruscan forms and was ornamented with terracotta antefixes. Where the Coliseum now stands we could at the same time admire Nero's vanished Golden House. On the Piazza of the Pantheon we should find not only the Pantheon of today, as it was bequeathed to us by Hadrian, but, on the same site, the original edifice erected by Agrippa; indeed, the same piece of ground would be supporting the church of Santa Maria Sopra Minerva and the ancient temple over which it was built. And the observer would perhaps only have to change the direction of his glance or position in order to call up the one view or the other. . . . The question may be raised why we chose precisely the past of a *city* to compare with the past of the mind. The assumption that everything past is preserved holds good even in mental life only on condition that the organ of the mind has remained intact and that its tissues have not been damaged by trauma or inflammation. But destructive influences which can be compared to causes of illness like these are never lacking in the history of a city. . . . Demolitions and replacements of buildings occur in the course of the most peaceful development of a city. . . . [I]t is rather the rule than the exception for the past to be preserved in mental life.[1]

[1] Sigmund Freud, *Civilisation and Its Discontents*, translated by James Strachey (New York: W. W. Norton, 1961), pp. 16–19.

I have decided to begin the discussion with this passage from Sigmund Freud because it captures the deepest essence of Rome, a city that can be likened to a mind, from which scraps of memory emerge that our feelings link to other memories and epochs. Its history is so intricate that it looks, at least at first glance, like an unfathomable jumble. Particularly striking is Freud's comparison of Rome with the timelessness of the unconscious. Simultaneously present in both are vast ruins and more modest constructions from the most diverse eras, and together they form a multilayered reality. In the city too, the preservation of the past—demolitions aside—is the rule, where different phases are phantasmagorically present, while those "change[s] . . . of glance" that Freud says would allow us to see all at once, in a timeless view, all the different stages of a building are today made possible by archaeological computer software.

Thus we live on top of meters and meters of accumulated memories lying invisible beneath concrete and asphalt, and they have influenced, literally from below, what still stands above them today: our urban life, in harmony or in contrast with what came before.

Recent studies have shown that conceiving the future is impossible without a memory of the past, because the same circuits of the mind that enable us to sail through our remembrances will color the backdrops of tomorrow. The past, on the other hand, is not only the residue that naturally remains;

it is also continually projected and re-projected by each present moment, much the same way we envision the days ahead of us. The urban stratifications filed away under our feet are thus only potentially a storehouse of data; they acquire meaning and value only in the reconstruction and narrative given them by the questions of our time.

I am an archaeologist, that is, a historian whose primary sources are things made by man. I am a peculiar sort of narrator, one who takes his cues from objects but who, in the process of reconstructing the past, later avails himself of every kind of source, including literary ones. The reconstruction of history, in fact, can only be a multivocal composition, with every voice bearing equal significance. The archaeologist, however, starts with structures and things. I certainly am not a bearer of absolute truths, which in any case are unattainable. Rather, I pose questions and propose solutions—that is, more or less plausible hypotheses whose results are provisional, the outcome of an attempt at synthesis that I am able to make today. As de Finetti writes, "everything is built on quicksand, though naturally one seeks to make the pillars rest on the relatively less dangerous points."[2]

[2] B. de Finetti, *L'invenzione della verità* (Milan: Raffaello Cortina, 2006).

In translating things into a narrative—especially as concerns the archaic and early-archaic periods—we must imagine ourselves not only as historians of a special kind, but also as *reges-augures*, *flamines*, and *pontifices*, that is, as kings and priests, men of religion as well as reason, because the first Romans firmly believed in their gods and the rituals they used to worship them. Law, politics, and the state—which were beginning to emerge at that time—were still enveloped in a sacred aura. Religion, morality, and politics had not yet become separate areas of life but were interconnected realities in the mind. The wise secular historian does not secularize a past steeped in sacredness but rather uses keen rational thought to understand phenomena originally imbued with theology, myth, and ritual, a sphere of pervasive and unifying emotions.

<hr />

It is not possible to understand the beginnings of a human settlement without retracing the urban history in reverse. A bit like what happens in the game of pick-up sticks: first one takes away the last sticks to fall, which cover others without being covered by them, and one proceeds in this fashion until all that is left is the last stick, which was the first to fall onto the table. The question I happen to ask most often of my collaborators during excavations is the following: "Which is the uncovered stratum to be excavated?" During twenty years of investigation of the land between the Palatine and the Forum, we have gone back over broad swaths of space and time, transforming the vast accumulation of surviving materials—the "stratification"—into a sequence of actions, activities, and events ordered over time and fathomed by human intelligence—"stratigraphy." Without stratigraphic culture and technology, one can dig up the ground in search of lost treasures, but one cannot unearth the memory of a city and reconstruct it analytically and as a whole. The digger is like a hunter who catches an animal by burning down the forest in which it dwells. The excavator, on the other hand, is more like a naturalist, who is interested in the forest overall and can observe a common plant, an insect, a mammal, or a gigantic tree with the same eye.

In this same spirit I would like to take the reader by the hand and have him or her descend with me some thirteen meters under the city of Rome—to where, atop the rubble and rubbish, the living settlements once grew, one on top of the other—and go back more than twenty-seven centuries into the past, in search of the first acts and the first day of Rome's existence: April 21, around 750 BC (fig. 1). What was born on that day? What events of importance for us and for world history followed over the millennia?

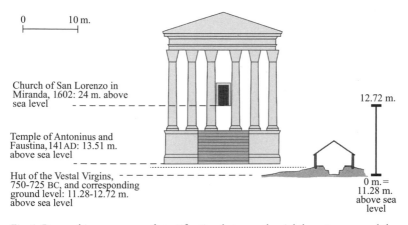

0   10 m.

Church of San Lorenzo in
Miranda, 1602: 24 m. above
sea level

12.72 m.

Temple of Antoninus and
Faustina, 141 AD: 13.51 m.
above sea level

Hut of the Vestal Virgins,
750-725 BC, and corresponding
ground level: 11.28-12.72 m.
above sea level

0 m. =
11.28 m.
above sea
level

Fig. 1. Rome, thirteen meters of stratification between the eighth century BC and the seventeenth century AD.

In Roman calendrical inscriptions one reads the words: *Roma condita*, that is, "Rome founded" (fig. 2). The exact year matters little—whether it is 753 BC or, as Roman historians maintained, a year between 758 and 725. What matters most is that Rome was born and created as a city and state between 775 and 675 BC, during the century to which tradition assigns the reigns of the three founding kings: the Latin Romulus and the Sabines Titus Tatius and Numa Pompilius.

The fundamental historical problem lies in determining whether the exploits of these three founding kings were in-

	MARTIVS	APRILIS	MAIVS	IVNIUS	QVINCTILIS
	I	II	III	IV	V
1	KAL. Iunoni Covellae (?);Iunoni Lucinae (?); Marti, ancilia moventur.	KAL. Iunoni Covellae (?).	KAL. Iunoni Covellae (?).	KAL. Iunoni Covellae (?); Marti extra portam Capenam (?).	KAL. Iunoni Covellae (?).
2					
3					
4					
5					POPLIFVGIA Iovi.
6					
7	NON. Vediovi inter duos lucos (?).	NON.	NON.	NON. Vesta aperitur; Dio Fidio in Colle (?).	NON. Nonae; Caprotinae (?); Romulus non apparuit (?).
8					
9	Ancilia moventur.		LEMVRIA Lemuribus.	VESTALIA Vestae.	
10					
11			LEMVRIA Lemuribus, Maniae	MATRALIA Matri Matutae.	
12					
13			LEMVRIA Lemuribus.		
14	EQVIRRIA Marti; Mamuralia (?).				
15	EID. Feriae Iovi; Annae Perennae.	EID. Feriae Iovi; FORDICIDIA Telluri Marti.	EID. Feriae Iovi; itur ad Argeos.	EID. Feriae Iovi; Vesta clauditur; Q.ST.D.F. (Quando stercus delatum, fas).	EID. Feriae Iovi.
16	Itur ad Argeos.				
17	LIBERALIA Libero, Liberae; AGONALIA Martia; itur ad Argeos.		Ambarvalia Deae Diae (?).		
18					
19	QVINQVATRUS Marti; ancilia moventur, saltatio saliorum in Comitio	CERIALIA Cereri.			LVCARIA.
20					
21		PARILIA Pali; Roma condita.	AGONALIA Vediovi (?).		LVCARIA.
22					
23	TUBILVSTRIUM Marti, ancilia moventur.	VINALIA (priora) Iovi.	TUBILVSTRIUM Volcano.		NEPTUNALIA Neptuno.
24	Q.R.C.F. (Quando Rex comitavit, fas).		Q.R.C.F. (Quando Rex comitavit, fas).		
25		ROBIGALIA Robigo.			FVRRINALIA Furrinae.
26					
27				Laribus (?); Iovi Statori (?).	
28					
29		***		***	
30	***		***		***

	SEXTILIS II = SEPTEMBER	SEPTEMBER II = NOVEMBER			
	SEXTILIS I = SEXTILIS	SEPTEMBER I= OCTOBER	OCTOBER = DECEMBER	NOVEMBER = IANUARIUS	DECEMBER = FEBRUARIUS
	VI	VII	VIII	IX	X
1	KAL. Iunoni Covellae (?).	KAL. Iunoni Covellae (?); Tigillo Sororio (?); Fidei (?).	KAL. Iunoni Covellae (?).	KAL. Iunoni Covellae (?).	KAL. Iunoni Covellae (?).
2					
3					
4					
5					
6					
7	NON. Saluti in Colle (?).	NON.	NON.	NON.	NON. Fornacalia.
8					
9				AGONALIA (Iano).	
10					
11		MEDITRINALIA Iovi.	AGONALIA INDI (GETI); Septimontium Palatuae (?).	CARMENTALIA Carmentae.	
12					
13		FONTINALIA Fonti.			Parentalia.
14					
15	EID. Feriae Iovi.	EID. Feriae Iovi; Iovi Feretrio (?); (September=) October equus Marti (?).	EID. Feriae Iovi; CONSUALIA Conso.	EID. Feriae Iovi; CARMENTALIA Carmenta.	EID. Feriae Iovi. LVPERCALIA Fauno Luperco.
16					
17	PORTVNALIA Portuno.		SATVRNALIA Saturno.		QVIRINALIA Quirino.
18					
19	VINALIA (rustica vel altera Iovi).	ARMILVSTRIVM Marti, ancilia moventur.	OPALIA Opi ad Forum.		
20					
21	CONSUALIA Conso.		DIVALIA Angeronae.		FERALIA dis inferis, Tacitae Mutae.
22					
23	VOLCANALIA Volcano, Horae Quirini, Maiae supra Comitium		LARENTALIA Accae Larentinae, Iovi.		TERMINALIA Termino.
24					REGIFVGIVM Iovi?.
25	OPICONSIVA Opi Consiviae in regia.				
26					
27	VOLTVRNALIA Volturo.				EQVIRRIA Marti.
28					
29	***		***		***
30		***		***	

Fig. 2. The Romulian ten-month calendar (reconstruction) and the day of the Parilia.

vented at a later date and projected back to the eighth century BC to ennoble the humble obscurity of the origins, as contemporary historians maintain, or whether we are dealing with realities that are part myth, part history—that is, "mythohistorical," in which the true is blended not so much with the false as with the fictive. Romulus being the son of Mars, for example, is clearly myth, whereas his deeds, as we shall see, are not merely legend.

To test whether these deeds were at their origin likely to have happened, we need testimonials outside the ancient literary tradition represented by Cicero, Livy, Dionysius of Halicarnassus, and Plutarch, on the one hand, and Varro and Verrius Flaccus, on the other. We need something that might allow us to evaluate the legend of Rome and reconstruct what objectively happened in the early days of the city.

Contemporary historians maintain, as a rule, that the city was not "founded" by anyone but "formed" gradually and anonymously. In their opinion, there was a city-state at Rome no earlier than the second half of the seventh century BC, at the time, that is, of Ancus Marcius and Tarquinius Priscus. In this way, the legend is reduced to a fable projected onto an entirely falsified eighth century BC.

Archaeologists, on the other hand—and, in particular, we who have been excavating in the heart of the city over the past twenty years, between the Palatine and the Forum (fig. 3)—maintain that the topography and stratigraphy now

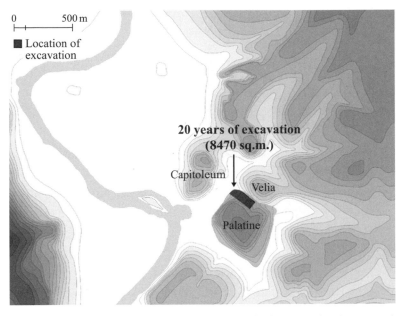

0   500 m
■ Location of
  excavation

**20 years of excavation
(8470 sq.m.)**

Capitoleum

Velia

Palatine

Fig. 3. One hectare of the Palatine excavated under the direction of Andrea Carandini.

provide very important data that coincide with the main events recounted in the saga of Remus, Romulus, and Titus Tatius. They both indicate achievements of a centralized nature, and public complexes for all the people that could only have been commissioned by and executed through the agency of a central authority: the first *rex-augur*, called Romulus.[3]

[3] Cf. A. Carandini, ed., *La leggenda di Roma*, vol. 1 (Milan: Mondadori, 2006).

An Epochal Event

In the long journey of humanity, the founding of Rome represents an epochal event that separates us from prehistory and inaugurates history. Let us follow, in broad stages, humanity's path through time.

Before 775/750 BC, which is the space of time considered by excavators to be the most likely period in which the city was founded, there were no cities or states in the Mediterranean of a more or less constitutional character. Indeed, the Minoan and Mycenaean centers in the Aegean were settlements that might well have served as capitals of states, but they had grown up around despotic foci of power. From 775/750 BC to the fifth–sixth centuries AD, in the western Mediterranean, and much later in the eastern Mediterranean, a world based on the "ancient" city-states was created—and then swallowed up by the Roman Empire. After the period of decadence of the Western cities between the fifth–sixth and tenth–eleventh centuries AD, during which protohistory seems to revive, the cities blossomed anew, never to fall again into decadence. A number of these cities achieved a degree of regional prominence, while others became centers and metropolises of large states. To this day, in Italy, the sense of the "nation"—still very young—is not deeply felt, and the same is true for the "region," while the identification with cities remains very strong—in stark contrast with other European countries, such as England and France, where great capitals and large kingdoms formed and then evolved into European nations. From this, one can deduce that without their substratum as Roman cities, the city-states and kingdoms of Europe would not have existed or would have been quite different.

Rome is just as old as Athens, which well qualifies it as the most ancient city-state and, moreover, as the most influential, having created a vast empire stretching from Portugal to Mesopotamia, from Germany to the Fezzan. In this city and its ecumenical power lie one of the principal roots of our identity, one that continues to inform our way of living, feeling, and thinking.

Let us continue the discussion by focusing our attention now on space. Because of the invention of the city-state around 775/750 BC, the Mediterranean and, later, Europe began to differentiate themselves increasingly from Asia and the East , the first sources of civilization. They created, in this way, their own unprecedented Western civilization, now in decline, whose bond to ancient Rome still remains. In the period immediately following World War II, there was a general desire to break free of this bond, owing to the ideological excesses of the Fascist and Nazi regimes. Today, however, we are in a position to rediscover this bond, free of any brutal abuse of politics.

In the East, the city and the state were centered around a fortified, "forbidden" palace, the court of an absolute ruler, and the despot made his decisions in this sumptuous dwelling (figs. 62 and 64). These circumstances did not favor the emergence of the sort of social body that can counterbalance royal sovereignty and that gives rise to the first embryonic forms of liberty: an aristocracy capable of constituting an opposition to royal power. In the West, by contrast, the "ancient" city-states were centered around not only the urban habitat but the elevated acropolis or citadel, on the one hand, and the agora or forum in the lower city, on the other, both of which constituted sacred and political centers of a *res publica*, or "public thing." And while the city-state, particularly at its origins, was upheld by a monarch, it nevertheless appears to have been of a "constitutional" nature (as Mommsen observed in the case of Rome). The house of the king, in fact, appears to have been rather modest, no more luxurious than was the norm for aristocratic dwellings (fig. 62). This would indicate a vested power limited by other governing bodies, such as a council of elders or plebian assembly. In short, the *res publica* or state was subjected, in the organization of the city, to a juridical and political ordering of a constitutional nature, one that was only periodically upset by tyrannies and dominations.

In French absolutism, the gap between the immensity of the Versailles of the court and the nobility's *hôtels* in the towns appears to be of the Eastern sort, but royal absolutism in Europe lasted only from the mid-seventeenth century until the Congress of Vienna. The prevalence of more or less constitutional organizations for much longer durations defines what we might call the Western syndrome, which arises from the invention of law and politics. The potent humus from which it grows—a stratum missing in other parts of the world—becomes the requirement of its ultimate result: democracy.[4]

The Site of Rome before Rome

The legend of Rome's founding, as recounted by historians and recorded in detail by scholars, is itself a great jumble— an amalgamation of mythical subjects and supposedly real events—that must be excavated stratigraphically if we are to go back from the later reconstructions to the earliest core of the narrative. The legend can most probably be dated around the time of the founding or shortly thereafter, between the mid-eighth and mid-seventh centuries BC.[5] As in all the myths of our world, it tells of something emerging from nothing. In so doing, it expresses at once a truth and a fiction. Indeed, the founding of Rome is without question the beginning of an epoch, but one that followed other important beginnings, and thus we can say that city does not arise out of nothing.

---

[4] Cf. A. Carandini, *Sindrome occidentale* (Genoa: Il Melangolo, 2007).

[5] Carandini, ed., *Leggenda di Roma*.

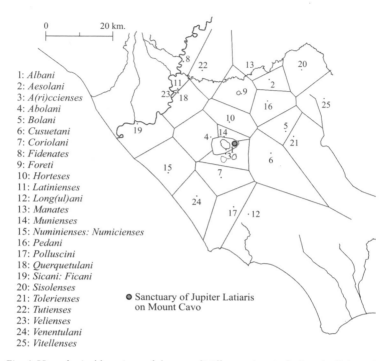

0   20 km.

1: *Albani*
2: *Aesolani*
3: *A(ri)ccienses*
4: *Abolani*
5: *Bolani*
6: *Cusuetani*
7: *Coriolani*
8: *Fidenates*
9: *Foreti*
10: *Horteses*
11: *Latinienses*
12: *Long(ul)ani*
13: *Manates*
14: *Munienses*
15: *Numinienses: Numicienses*
16: *Pedani*
17: *Polluscini*
18: *Querquetulani*
19: *Sicani: Ficani*
20: *Sisolenses*
21: *Tolerienses*
22: *Tutienses*
23: *Velienses*
24: *Venentulani*
25: *Vitellenses*

◉ Sanctuary of Jupiter Latiaris
   on Mount Cavo

Fig. 4. Hypothetical locations of the *populi Albenses* (not including the Bubetani, Macrales, Octulani, Olliculani, Vimitellani).

Here the myth does not so much sublimate as obscure a prior reality, which we are, however, in a position to reconstruct. Indeed, the site of Rome, particularly Mount Saturnius, later called the Capitolium, had been consistently inhabited from the first half of the second millennium BC and later grew and spread out in various phases before becoming a city.

At the end of the second millennium began the world that is of most immediate interest to us: that of the first Latins and their oddly named communities, listed by Pliny the Elder, which represented as many *populi* settled in villages (fig. 4). The metropolis of these federated Latins at the time was Alba Longa, situated along the edge of the volcanic lake at the foot of Mons Albanus, today called Monte Cavo (fig. 5). At the top of the mountain, the people worshipped Jupiter Latiaris (Iuppiter Latialis), the highest deity of Latium, the territory of the ancient Latins, which was separated from the Etruscans by the Tiber River and from the Sabines by a boundary

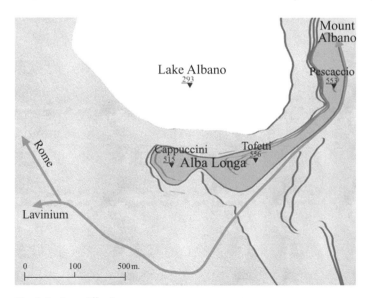

Fig. 5. Latium, Alba Longa.

beyond the Aniene River (see fig. 59). This account, which can be found in literary sources and has its archaeological counterpart in a "pre-urban" settlement made up of scattered villages, has been generally accepted by contemporary historians. A few of these thirty communities can be ascribed to the site that will become Rome (fig. 6), centered around a ford in the Tiber a short distance downstream from the Isola Tiberina, at the foot of the Aventine, where Ancus Marcius would build the Pons Sublicius. Through this point passed the "salt route"—the Via Salaria and the Via Campana—salt being, of course, an essential element of food and its preservation (fig. 7). This is the first reality that the saga of the city's founding obscures.

The above settlements were followed by a new kind—one not taken into account by contemporary historians—which consisted of a large village or center that the pre-urban villages of the location had absorbed and transcended. The archaeologists who discovered this have defined it as "proto-urban." It stood at the center of its territory, from which it seems to have been kept quite distinct, and was considerable in size for the time. In the first half of the ninth century BC, this center was divided into two blocs: that of the *montes* (mounts), called the Septimontium, and that of the *colles* (hills), whose name is not known to us. But already by the second half of the same century, these two blocs had merged into a single entity through the initiative or imposition of the more pow-

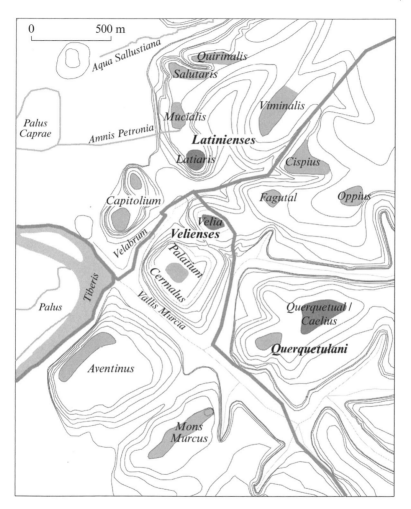

Fig. 6. The three *populi Albenses* of the site of Rome: Latinienses, Velienses, Querquetulani.

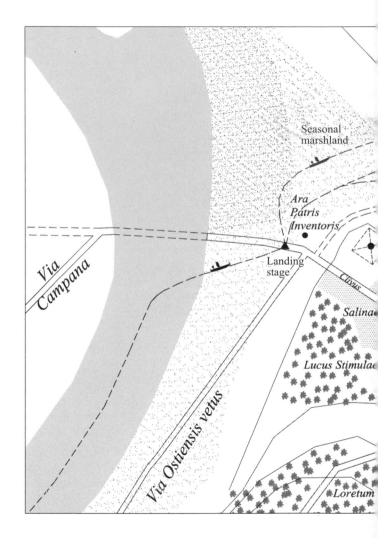

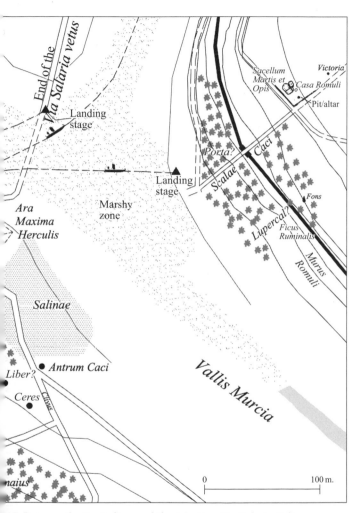

. 7. Between the Capitolium and the Aventine: Via Salaria, Salinae,
1 Via Campana

erful of the two: the Septimontium. Indeed, quite likely the *montes* incorporated the *colles*. The result was the enlarged Septimontium cited by Varro (fig. 8). This is the second reality obscured by the saga of the city's founding.

The unitary proto-urban settlement of the site of Rome—about 205 hectares (*montes*, 139 hectares; *colles*, 65 hectares)—is scarcely larger than that of Veii (about 190 hectares). It drove the necropoles—which had previously been located in the valleys between prominences—out to the peripheries, and its neighborhoods (*curiae*) seem quite distinct from the districts and partitions of the *ager*[6] (fig. 59) of which it constituted the center. The more vulnerable part of this center could be protected by moats, the Fossae Quiritium. At its origin, Rome was not much greater in size (241 hectares). For this reason, the founding of the city is not so striking from a quantitative as from a qualitative perspective—that is, for the invention of a new form of organization and government. The relationship between the *agri* of Rome and Veii is inverted with respect to that of the two urban centers: Veii's territory was five times greater than that of Rome (fig. 9).

The scholars of ancient Rome, who didn't have any mythohistorical overview but were simply very curious about rare details, as scholars always are, have revealed to us the name

---

[6] Translator's note: The land surrounding a city, used chiefly for farming.

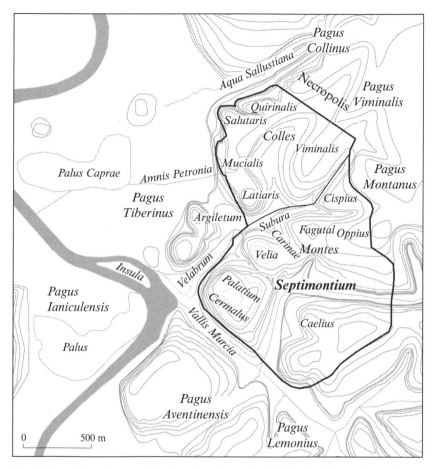

Fig. 8. The *colles* and *montes* (the Septimontium of Antistius Labeo) that make up the greater Septimontium of Varro. *Montes*, 139 hectares; *colles*, 65 hectares; Septimontium, 205 hectares.

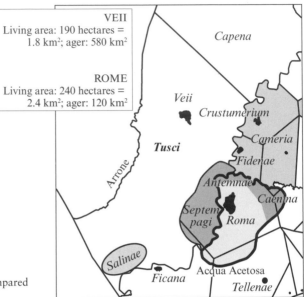

VEII
Living area: 190 hectares =
1.8 km²; ager: 580 km²

ROME
Living area: 240 hectares =
2.4 km²; ager: 120 km²

Capena

Veii

Crustumerium

Tusci

Cameria

Fidenae

Arrone

Antemnae

Caenina

Septem pagi

Roma

Salinae

Ficana

Acqua Acetosa

Tellenae

Fig. 9. Rome compared with Veii.

of the realities that immediately preceded the establishment of Rome: Septimontium. As is clear from the name, this is a unitary aggregate of mounts (*montes*) and, later, of mounts incorporating hills, sometime before roughly 775 BC. These mounts and hills were in turn divided into family-related associations of men within districts or neighborhoods in the settlements; these were called *curiae* (from **co-viriae*) and protected by the local god Quirinus (from **Co-virinus*).

These men were called Quirites (from *Co-virites*), the Latin inhabitants of the site, and were much more ancient than the Romans, the latest arrivals. The neighborhoods of the Quirites therefore existed before the city of the Romans.[7] Yet contemporary historians, disagreeing with Varro, continue to date the Septimontium during the first royal era, thus after 775 BC, and to consider the *curiae* as an invention of the city and not of the proto-city. The Septimontium, however, first being limited to the *montes* and then including the *colles*, reflects the reality of the proto-urban center—which historians ignore—not the urban center, as evidenced by the fact that it is a noncentralized aggregate of neighborhoods.

The settlement and territory of the Septimontium had probably already been inhabited for a century before the establishment of a city by common families and hegemonic groups (*gentes*), along with the subordinate group (*clientes*) that worked their lands. Over the course of the ninth century BC, the inhabitants had moved from a primitive social parity toward an initial, embryonic division of society into the governors and the governed. It was the *patres* and elders of the *gentes* who led the great proto-urban center on the Tiber. At the time there was no central power vested in a king; nor were there any central, public places, but only partitions of which the Palatium—the northern section of the Palatine—was a

[7] A. Carandini, *Remo e Romolo: Dai rioni dei Quiriti alla città dei Romani* (Turin: Einaudi, 2006).

mons primus inter pares. This is not the understanding of contemporary historians, who have the *gentes* arising with the establishment of the city, in contradiction with the archaeological evidence that emerges from the necropoles (particularly that of Osteria dell'Osa, which was one of those of Gabii.)

If, before Rome, there indeed existed a proto-urban center as large as the inhabited area of early Rome, what could Romulus have done of any originality in founding the city? We shall see shortly. First, we must form a summary idea of the area of Rome as subdivided into a variety of eminences. This works for the villages but creates problems when considering a unitary, centralized settlement, which in the best of cases would be situated on a plateau, as in the case of Veii. Nevertheless, the ford of the Tiber at the foot of the Aventine was so important that it was impossible to abandon that problematic group of eminences.

The mounts and hills of Rome define a space that, had it been flat, would not now be distinguishable in its various parts. In Rome, however, everyone still calls the mounts by their original names, and the Viminal for us remains the same eminence that the first Romans designated by that name. Only between the Fagutal and the Oppius has there been some confusion, one that, however, can be easily dispelled by returning to the correct traditional theory according to which the Fagutal lies close to the Velia at San Pietro in Vincoli, and the Oppius between the Caelius and the Cispius, culminating where the Palazzo Brancaccio now stands.[8]

According to the order handed down to us by Verrius Flaccus in the work of Sextus Pompeius Flaccus, the *montes* consisted of the Palatium, Velia, Fagutal, Subura, Cermalus, Oppius, Caelius, and Cispius. The *colles* were made up of the Latiaris, Mucialis, Salutaris, Quirinalis, and Viminalis. The Mons Saturnius—the future Capitolium/Arx[9]—was connected to the Latiaris by a saddle, while the eminence of the Aventinus was separated from the Cermalus/Palatium or Palatine by the Vallis Murcia, where the Circus Maximus would later be built (fig. 9).

The Places of Rome

The legend of Rome barely touches upon the Quirites settlement as a whole and never mentions the Septimontium. Indeed, Rome had to have arisen from nothingness so that Romulus's achievement could appear to have happened without prior groundwork and constitute a miracle: the founding.

---

[8] M. C. Capanna and A. Amoroso, "Velia, Fagutal, Oppius. Il periodo archaico e le case di Servio Tullio e Tarquinio Prisco," in *Workshop di Archeologia Classica* 3 (2006): 87–111. The boundary between the *colles* Salutaris and Quirinalis is similarly controversial.

[9] An arx was a Roman citadel. As an arx was built very early on the Capitoline hill, or Capitolium, the latter was often referred to as the Arx.—Trans.

This "founding," in fact, involved not the realization of any plans for a city but a series of ceremonial acts and sacred prohibitions that instilled into the soil and the people a will to power expressed from the start in forms that we might term "modern"—that is, juridical, political, governmental, constitutional—masked but not negated by sacred and holy institutions. For this reason, the date of April 21, sometime around 750 BC, is an important one, in that it is the day of the initial ceremony that inaugurated cults, rites, and institutions in public places for functions henceforth centralized and no longer limited to the home, neighborhood, or district. Thus arose a project that would come to be realized over the second half of the eighth century BC. The acts of the founding kings were therefore centered around several of the city's mythic sites, those most profoundly transformed by the spatial and human organization of the city-state: on the one hand, the Aventine and Palatine; on the other, the Forum and the Capitolium/Citadel. The remaining, uninaugurated habitat of the Quirites is implied in the legend by a number of events that took place on other mounts and hills, and by the thirty neighborhoods or *curiae* that Romulus instituted and that—given their great number—could not be included in the Palatine (fig. 10).

Contemporary historians have refuted the thesis of the founding of the city around the mid-eighth century BC— that is, the idea that it was created in a very short time—

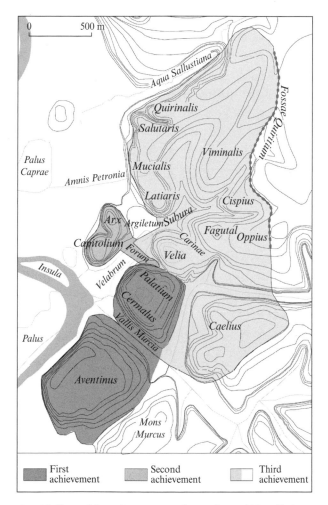

Fig. 10. Sites of the achievements of Romulus and Titus Tatius.

preferring the notion of a "formation" which they believe took place over a longer and more recent period of time. And since they see the city as coming into existence only around 600 BC, the entire era of the first kings—Romulus, Numa Pompilius, Tullus Hostilius, and Ancus Marcius—is considered to have laid the groundwork for the future city and made to coincide with the Septimontium. If, however, we posit the founding and realization of the city in the second half of the 8th century BC, as the Romans believed and as excavators in the heart of the city today also believe, then the Septimontium must of necessity be dated back to the period from 850 to 750 BC, as suggested by Varro, who considered it as predating Romulus.

The Aventine and the Palatine had chiefs in primordial times: first Cacus, enemy of Hercules, who killed him; then the aboriginal kings Picus, Faunus, and Latinus, descendents of Mars who frequented the Mons Murcus and are present in the Lupercal in the famous Bolsena mirror (figs. 7 and 12); and finally, Faustulus, the putative parent, with Acca Larentia, of Remus and Romulus, who appears as a local chieftain, an earthly manifestation of Faunus, as his name would imply (fig. 12). It was on the rural Aventine that observations of the flights of birds, which revealed divine will, were to take place, as well as the rites that prepared the foundation of the city and made Romulus king. The Palatine was the site of bird observations related to the consecration or inauguration of that hill, thanks to which the hilly terrain became an *urbs* (city) called Roma Quadrata—at once the royal citadel and the symbolic heart (*pars pro toto*) of the entire settlement, established on the quadrangular Mons Palatinus. This was Romulus's first achievement (fig. 10).

The Forum and the Capitolium/Arx —a rural district *super partes* at the southern edge of the settlement—were the sites where the ceremonies would be held and where the public places of the sacred and political center of the *res publica*, or state, would be instituted. This was Romulus's second achievement, carried out this time together with the Sabine Titus Tatius (fig. 10).

Although by killing Remus, Romulus had reduced the duality of twinhood to the unity of monarchy, the compromise with the Sabines—who neither defeated the Romans nor were defeated by them—led to a dual royalty and renewed the prevalence of duality over singularity, a concept that would find its grandest, most durable manifestation in the Republican consuls, who were like dual kings for a year.

From the northeast corner of the Palatine, site of the communal meals of the *curiae*, the Quirites would be (re)organized into thirty neighborhoods; just as the calendar (fig. 2), comprising ten months, would be (re)organized from the Capitol and the urban territory divided into three parts, or *tribus* (fig. 59). People, time, and space would be governed by a king assisted and limited by an ensemble of bodies: a priestly order, a royal council, and a people's assembly. But only the king—characterized as *potentissimus*—would hold sovereignty, as moderated by the lesser powers. This was the *constitutio Romuli*, Romulus's third achievement, perfected with Titus Tatius. The first achievement of the inaugurated, walled Palatine—better known because it is associated with the founding date of April 21—has no meaning if disassociated from the other two. All were integral parts of a single project of foundation.

While the proto-urban center, or Septimontium, and later the developed area of Rome, were larger than the Etruscan Veii, the original area of Rome appears to have been much smaller—only one-fifth that of Veii (fig. 9). This points to an inability to grow on the part of the proto-urban center and helps explain the need for the bloody transition to city-state. The new entity immediately set about expanding, thanks to the citizen army, and quickly reached and surpassed Veii during the reign of the fourth king, Ancus Marcius (figs. 60–61). We do not know the Quirites settlement in its entirety, especially the northern end, but we can reconstruct its boundaries (for now) by elimination, based on the space left over from the necropoles that surrounded it between the Esquiline and the Quirinal. The Esquiline would later be extended by Servius Tullius (fig. 11). The dead were moved away from the living much sooner in Rome than in Athens.

Remus and Romulus and the
Kings of Alba Longa

In Latium and Rome, miraculous births were the province not of single heroes but of twins, usually friendly to each other, though they sometimes became enemies over time, as in the case of Remus and Romulus. Other twins include the Lares, who worked together and protected the boundaries of the inhabited space ever since primordial times. Remus and Romulus were sons of a known mother, Acca Larentia, and an uncertain father, an unlikely, late-coming Mercury, behind whom probably hid the divine forebear Mars, who had already sired the aboriginal kings (the Aborigines had come down into Latium from the region of Reate, the modern Rieti). These kings were Picus the woodpecker and Faunus the wolf, who with his brother Latinus was associated with a sow that gave birth to thirty piglets—the thirty peoples of Latium. Mentioned even by Hesiod in the *Theogony* at the end of the eighth century BC, these brothers are considered founders of the Latin people. Often associated with animals—like Australian totems—these deities were later obscured after the Trojan heroes Aeneas and Ascanius were introduced into Latin mythology around the sixth century BC as founders of Roman civilization (as attested by the image of an "inspection with libation" archaeologically discovered in the "tumulus of Aeneas" at Lavinio).

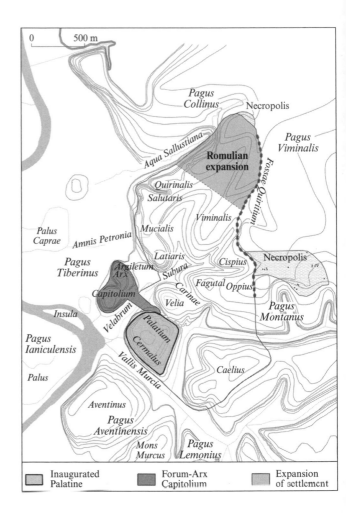

0   500 m

*Pagus
Collinus*   Necropolis

Aqua Sallustiana

**Romulian
expansion**

*Pagus
Viminalis*

Fossae Quiritium

*Quirinalis
Salutaris*

Viminalis

*Palus
Caprae*

Mucialis

Amnis Petronia

*Pagus
Tiberinus*

Latiaris

*Argiletum
Arx*

Subura

Cispius

Necropolis

Capitolium

Fagutal Oppius

Carinae

Insula

Velabrum

Velia

*Pagus
Montanus*

*Pagus
Ianiculensis*

*Palatium
Cermalus*

Palus

Vallis Murcia

Caelius

Aventinus

*Pagus
Aventinensis*

*Mons
Murcus*

*Pagus
Lemonius*

| | Inaugurated Palatine | | Forum-Arx Capitolium | | Expansion of settlement |

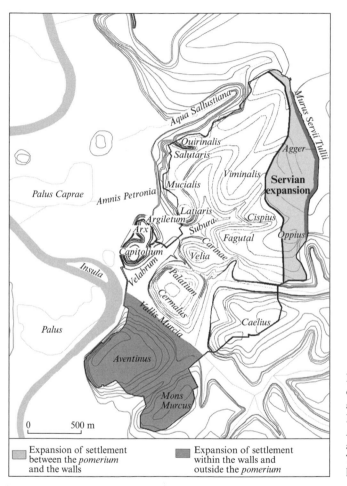

Fig. 11. The Rome of Romulus (settled area, 241 hectares; Forum–Capitolium/ Arx, 12.8 hectares) and that of Servius Tullius (361.9 hectares).

Succeeding the aboriginal kings of Latium are the Silvi, who issued from Silvius, the founder of the line. They are followed by a lacuna in the cultural memory of the Latins—later filled with artificial names—but in the end, the authentic names of the last sovereigns reemerge: Procas and his sons and successors, that is, the perfidious Amulius and the good Numitor. Numitor had a daughter, whom he himself "took" as priestess of Vesta to tend the royal hearth at Alba Longa. One day, this sacred hearth sprouted a phallus, also of the god Mars, who proceeded to possess the princess. From this union between the virgin priestess and the god of spring—the name March derives from Mars—a pair of twins were born (fig. 12). The firstborn was Remus, who is always named first by the Romans, the second-born Romulus, always named second and, moreover, called Atellus, that is, the diminutive *alter* ("other") with respect to a *primus*.

As concerns the name Romulus, we find help in linguistics, according to which it is not a late coinage, in which case the founder would have been called Romanus; nor does it mean "the Roman," as contemporary historians have believed. Rather, it is the name of a person of Etruscan roots and can be dated no later than the sixth century BC and more likely to the seventh/eighth centuries BC. Moreover, it has the same root as *Rome*.[10] It is important to recall that in myths the

---

[10] See, on this subject, the arguments of the linguist C. de Simone in Carandini, ed., *Leggenda di Roma*.

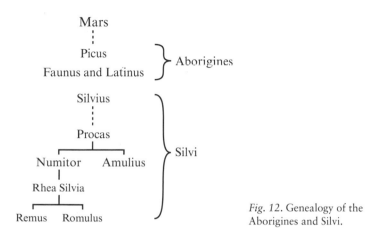

Mars
⋮
Picus
Faunus and Latinus
} Aborigines

Silvius
⋮
Procas
┌────┴────┐
Numitor   Amulius
│
Rhea Silvia
┌────┴────┐
Remus   Romulus

} Silvi

Fig. 12. Genealogy of the Aborigines and Silvi.

world over, it is usually the second-born who enjoys good fortune, as in the case of Jacob, who gains the Promised Land, while the firstborn Esau is forced to expatriate. According to one variant, Esau dies, like Remus, while attacking the citadel of his brother.[11]

The theological reality of the sons of Rhea Silvia is represented on the back of a mirror from Bolsena from the fourth century BC, the oldest known portrayal of the twins. Even more ancient, from the mid-fifth century, is the Capitoline she-wolf, which is exceptionally lifelike in its rendering of the animal's anatomy and swollen teats. Missing, however, are the twins, who were added later on, during the Renais-

---

[11] A. Carandini, *Archeologia del mito* (Turin: Einaudi, 2002).

sance (one restorer of this wolf claimed that it was a medieval bronze, but her conclusion is not convincing, since medieval animals look like little monsters and have nothing realistic about them).

But let us return to the Bolsena mirror (fig. 13): In the Lupercal cave at the foot of Palatine where the twins were raised and near to which Rome was to be founded, Remus and Romulus appear between the legs of the nursing she-wolf, a personification of Fauna (below is what is probably a wolf and personification of Faunus). Remus is looking at the she-wolf's head, while Faunus, the god of disorder, stands to the left of the scene; Romulus looks in the opposite direction, toward a regal figure holding a lance on the right, probably Latinus, founder of the Latin people, who points at Romulus, indicating his foreordainment as founder of Rome, thus making his mortal conflict with Remus seem predestined from the start. Behind and above them—so that it can be seen—is the desiccated relic of the Ficus Ruminalis, where two birds are perched, probably the woodpecker of Mars and the owl (*parra*) of Vesta, which allude to the twins' parents: the god of war and the vestal virgin Rhea Silvia. Above the Lupercal, in the spot where the literary sources place the Tugurium Faustuli et Accae, appear the father (in the guise of Mercury) and mother of the Lares. The brothers Faunus and Latinus stand for the pre-civic Lares of the Latins, just as Remus and

Fig. 13. The Bolsena mirror representing the Lupercal, 350–325 BC.

Romulus serve as the new civic Lares of the Romans. Not present—strangely enough, given the date of the mirror—is Aeneas. For this reason, the representation remains faithful to the most ancient stratum of the saga of Rome's origins (dating prior to the start of the sixth century BC), and thus bears witness to the most ancient, most authentic indigenous mythical tradition, which apparently, in the Middle Republic, survived alongside the tradition of Trojan heroes that the city had preferred to that of the divine kings of the Aborigines, considered too primitive in flavor.

THE PALATINE

-------- ❦ --------

The Preliminary Rite on the Aventine

The legend tells that Remus and Romulus were authorized by their grandfather, Numitor—whom they themselves had restored to the throne of Alba Longa—to found a city at the frontiers of Latium, at the ford in the Tiber River, where the twins had been raised by the she-wolf/Fauna and Acca Larentia. The kings of Alba, starting with the aboriginal Picus, the founder of the line, enjoyed the privilege of consulting birds to know the will of Jupiter and obtain his blessing. Thus they were *reges* as well as *augures*—in the *Aeneid*, Virgil has Picus sitting down, wearing a small *trabea*, holding the *lituus* of the augurs in his right hand, and the shield/*ancile* of the Saliens in his left. As princes of the ruling Alban house and authorized by Numitor, Remus and Romulus also enjoyed this privilege of the Silvi, whereby they studied the flight of birds to elicit Jupiter's favor. Remus climbed the Mons Murcus (or Minor Aventine) and Romulus the (Major) Aventine—according to Ennius—to learn from the auspice if they had the right to found a city on that site by the Tiber, on what day it should be founded, who should be its king, what name it should take, and on what soil it should be built. Should the omen be favorable, the winner was to ask Jupiter to "inaugurate" him, that is, to be consecrated as king, so that he could proceed to found the *urbs* (fig. 14). As we see, the preliminary rites took place in locations of a rural character, close to but outside the Palatine, where the initiations into adulthood were held for the Quirites of the proto-urban center (see the later cults to Liber and Minerva on the Aventine).

In order to probe the will of the gods and obtain blessings that brought with them irreversible changes in status, one needed to create an enclosed area (*templum*) about ten meters by ten, marked by nine inscribed cippi; the one to the northeast bore the words *bene iuvante ave*, indicating the most favorable bird-flight (fig. 15). The augur would sit at the center of the western side of the enclosure and look eastward to the horizon, where loomed the Mons Albans with its cult of Jupiter Latiaris. In the space encompassed by his field of vision, the pattern marked in the enclosure by the cippi was ideally projected onto the landscape, as the staff/horn (*lituus*; see fig. 16) moved in the air. If the birds were flying in from the northwest, full authorization was given, along with the gods' blessing. Remus placed the *templum* on the *saxum* (stone) of the Mons Murcus, in the spot where Numa was to meet Picus and Faunus, and where the church of Santa Balbina now stands. Romulus placed the *templum* at the top of the Aventine, where Sant'Alessio now stands, a church built over the Temple of Minerva (fig. 17). Tradition has it that

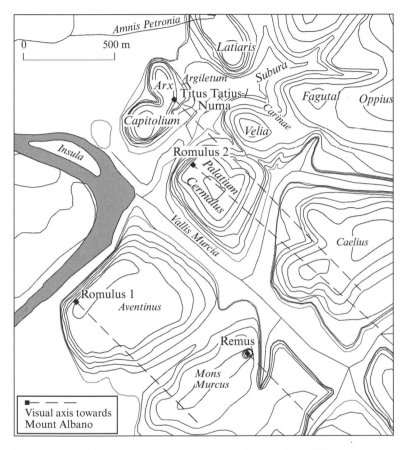

Fig. 14. First auspices of Remus and Romulus on the Aventine and the Mons Murcus. Second auspice of Romulus on the Palatine. Auspices of Titus Tatius (?) and Numa on the Capitolium (cf. fig. 17).

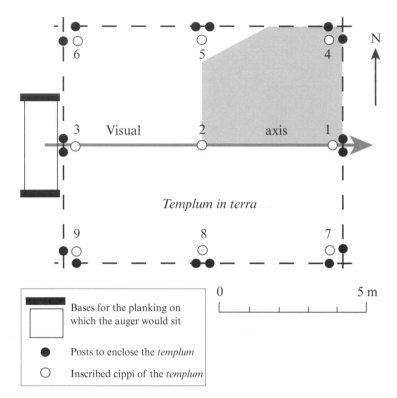

Fig. 15. Bantia (Potenza province), observatory for bird flights with inscribed cippi which read (1) Iovi; (2) Solei; (3) Flus(ae); (4) B(ene) iu(vante) a(ve); (5) T(——) a(ve) a(rcula?); (6) C(ontraria) av(e) a(uspicium) p(estiferum); (7) Sin(ente) av(e); (8) R(emore) ave; (9) C(ontraria) a(ve) en(ebra). Early first century BC.

Fig. 16. Latium, Gabii, augur holding the *lituus*, late archaic era.

Fig. 17. The auspices of Romulus and Remus between the Aventine and the Mons Murcus (cf. fig. 14).

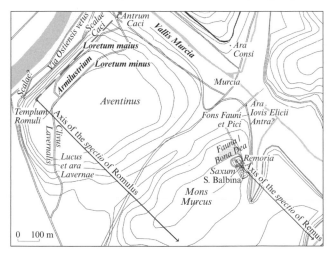

at dawn—the most propitious moment for observing birds—
Romulus obtained a more favorable auspice than Remus, for
which he was consecrated king; he chose to found the city on
the Palatine on April 21 and to call it Rome. From the double
auspices of Remus and Romulus, we glean that the idea of
founding a regnum governed by a single king was a choice
made by the twins before the auspices. Remus would have
wanted to found his settlement, called Remora or Remoria,
on the (Major) Aventine or even a bit farther away, where the
EUR district is now located (fig. 59). He therefore wanted the
settlement to be built in a specific part of the outlying countryside (*ager*), away from the proto-urban center. Romulus
instead wanted to found a city on the Palatine, in the very
heart of the proto-urban center—an innovative choice, since
this implied the conquest and spiritual and juridical transfor-
mation of the symbolic center of the Septimontium spanning
two *montes*: the Palatium and the Cermalus.

Once the founding was completed with the institution of
the Forum and the Capitolium/Arx, the kings would be inaugurated in the state's central *templum* on the Arx, probably beginning from the time of Titus Tatius—who made his
home there—and definitely during the reign of Numa Pompilius (fig. 14). The twins must have concluded their initiation
on December 15, which in the primitive ten-month calendar
was the feast of the Lupercalia. The action against Alba and
the killing of Amulius can be supposed to have occurred in

the second half of the same month. We can ascribe the first auspices to the new year's day of that same calendar, March 15; after which the war campaign began on March 23, on the feast of the Tubilustria. This is the date on which we can place Romulus's declaration of war on the Septimontium by hurling a lance of cornelian cherrywood from the Aventine toward the southern slope of the Palatine (Cermalus) (fig. 18): the lance lodged at the edge of the Stairs of Cacus, where it miraculously turned into a verdant tree. The site is located in front of the hut of Acca Larentia and the pig herder Faustulus, the earthly representative of Faunus and pre-civic chief of the place where the twins were raised (fig. 19). The miracle of the cornelian lance that reblooms manifests the gods' consent with the conquest achieved by Romulus and his band of young men, and with the founding of the *urbs* Roma Quadrata.

Just as we have imagined the first auspices-auguries on the Aventine on the first day of the "agrarian" new year, the auspice-augury on the Palatine also received divine authorization on a different new year's day, the one that immediately follows: the "pastoral" new year on April 21. This was the feast day of Parilia (from *parere*, "to give birth"), on which the goddess Pales was worshipped. On that day, the purification rites of humans and ovines were celebrated, which entailed jumping over fires, a custom believed propitious to the birth of goats. And the much-awaited, felicitous moment of

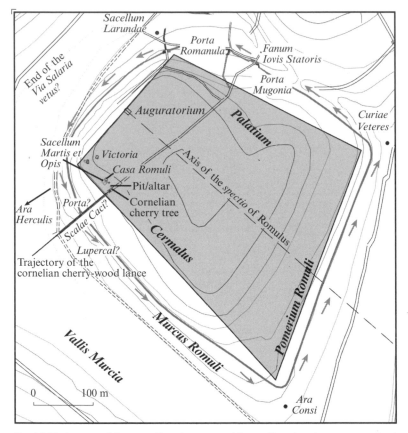

Fig. 18. Trajectory of the cornelian cherry-wood lance. *Templum* (or *auguratorium*) of the second auspices. Limit of the inaugurated Palatine (in grey) or *pomerium*. Counterclockwise path of the *sulcus primigenius* and walls.

Fig. 19. Scene of the Lupercal. Imaginary depiction with Latinus, the woodpecker, the ficus ruminalis, the she-wolf, the twins, Faustulus, Acca Larentia, and, at the top, their hut. (Studio Inklink)

the suckling lambs was near. It was on such an April day that Rome, according to unanimous traditions, was founded as a *civitas* and regnum—a city-state—and thus it constitutes the symbolic beginning of an era involving the new settlement of lands on the left bank of the Tiber, since on the right lay the *ager* of the Etruscan Veii, likely the ideal and practical model, first for the Septimontium and later for Rome itself. Indeed Romulus sent for priests from Etruria, from whom he learned how to found an *urbs* (which implies the prior foundation of *urbes* on the right bank of the Tiber). These priests must have introduced the king to the *libri rituales*, an Etruscan manual on urban foundations based on walls deemed holy (*sanctae*, that is, inviolable), on civic institutions (*tribus, curiae*) in harmony with the city plans, and on an army formally instituted to reflect the community.

The Blessing of the Palatine and the Founding of Roma Quadrata

On April 21, before dawn, Romulus stepped out of the hut in which he lived. To do what? Nearby was another hut, with two rooms, which might have been for the worship of Mars and Ops, the goddess of opulence (fig. 20). The two huts were built on a site where there had previously been one bigger hut, the archaeological correlative of that of Acca and

Faustulus (fig. 21). After making his sacrifice, the king most likely went to the center of the western slope of the Palatine and there created a second *templum* from which to observe bird flights—this, too, facing the Mons Albanus (fig. 18). First, he defined the boundaries, at the foot of the mount, within which he hoped the divine blessing (*augurium*, from *augere*, "to augment") would descend: a blessing analogous to the one he himself received on the Aventine, leading to his becoming king. He then marked these boundaries, starting at the four corners of the mount, having boundary stones implanted in the earth to demarcate the *pomerium*, or continuous border to be imagined behind the walls that would be later built. In the king-augur's vision, this represented the view onto the future *urbs* (fig. 22b). His gaze then continued, however, as far as the horizon, so that before his eyes, just beyond the *pomerium*, lay a view onto the *ager*, that is, the territory as far as Alba Longa (fig. 22c). At daybreak he received another favorable flight of birds, which indicated to him that the requested blessing had been granted. If the entire *ager* was *effatus* and *liberatus*, the Palatine was also *inauguratus* as a temple, except that the mount was not consecrated to any god. With the augury, the Palatine's status was elevated well above that of the other mounts and hills of the remaining settlement. Indeed, only the royal citadel on the Palatine—a symbolic microcosm of the entire settlement—was transformed into an *urbs*.

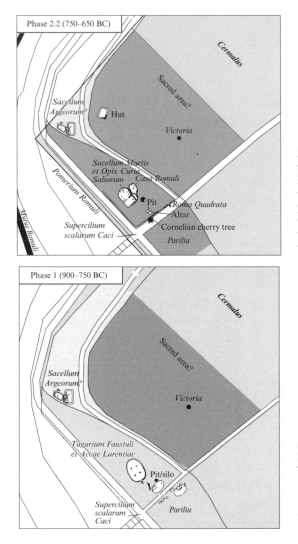

Fig. 20. Corner of the Palatine toward the Tiber. Romulus's hut together with that of the cults of Mars and Ops; pit (*fossa*) with altar (Roma Quadrata); cornelian cherry tree; and site of the feast of the Parilia.

Fig. 21. Corner of the Palatine toward the Tiber. The (chieftain's?) proto-urban hut is the archaeological correlative of the hut of Faustulus and Acca Larentia.

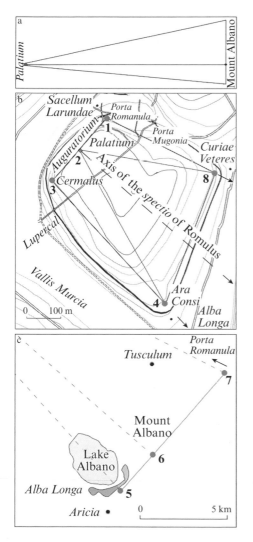

Fig. 22. (a) The royal *templum in aere* between the Palatine and Mount Albanus. (b) View of the Palatine/*Urbs*. (c) View of the *ager* as far as the horizon. The different numbers refer to the limits of the *templum in aere*, as reconstructed according to the the bronze tablets of Gubbio: (1) *angulus summus*; (2) *auguratorium/templum in terra* (*minus*), reconstructed on the basis of the *templum* of Bantia; (3) western corner, corresponding to corner no. 1; (4) limit of the southern boundary of the *pomerium*; (5) *angulus imus*; (6) *signum* of the *spectio* (*Mons Albanus*); (7) eastern corner, corresponding to corner no. 5; (8) limit of the northern boundary of the *pomerium*.

Concluding the augury, the feast of the Parilia, sacred to Pales, a goddess of the place similar to Fauna, was held in a primitive meeting-place in front of the royal hut—where the residence of Augustus, the new Romulus, would later stand. The feast celebrated the birthing season of the goats, the time of curds and cheese and spring lambs, when men and herds were purified by fire and sacred substances (fig. 20).

The members of the community would toss their first fruits and clods of their own earth—perhaps from the rural *pagi* and the *curiae* of the settlement— into a pit in front of Romulus's hut, in order to unify the parts by concealing them underground. Here we have the *condere* (literally, "to hide," whose root we find in the English "abscond" and "re-condite"), which ritually means "to found." Romulus himself was to be quartered, buried, and hidden in the ground; not in one pit, but presumably in many, perhaps one per *curia*, so that, as with Osiris and the Buddha, each district might possess a relic of the founder. An altar was then erected beside the pit, upon which a new fire was lit—a royal fire, since it was received into a hearth in the royal hut (fig. 23), though it was already starting to belong to everyone, considering the first fruits and different soils brought together in it. This represented an eclipsing of the cult of Cacus in favor of what seems to have been a proto-cult of Vesta, the definitive public worship of whom would later take place in the Forum. To the sounds of the trumpet-staff (*lituus*), the king would invoke the names of the *urbs*: the initiatory name, Amor; the sacred name, Flora; and the political name, Roma (Quadrata). So believed the scholars of ancient Rome. "Romulus" and "Roma" have a common root. The political name of the *urbs* finds confirmation in that of the eponymous gate of the Palatine called the Porta Romanula (fig. 18). We know that the gates could get their names from a circumstance inside the walls, as

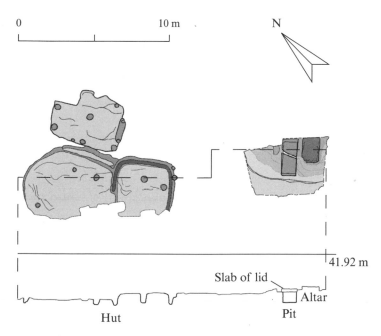

Fig. 23. The pit with the altar of the foundation (cf. fig. 18).

with the Quirinal gate in the Servian walls, named for the cult of Quirinus established on that hill.

The final ritual of the city's first day still remained to be performed. Romulus probably went to the northwest corner of the mount, where stood the Sacellum of Larunda—another name for Acca Larentia—just beyond the *pomerium*. This point represents a foundational corner (*summus*) of the *templum*, which the founder had delineated *in aere*, based on the one *in terra*, which corresponded to the other foundational corner (*imus*), situated at Alba Longa. Here, the king, wearing a toga in the manner of the Gabii that covered his head (*cinctus Gabinus*), initiated the Etruscan rite of the *sulcus primigenius* ("first furrow"), just learned from the Etruscan priests who had been summoned (from nearby Veii?) for the occasion.

To a plough with a ritual bronze ploughshare, Romulus yoked a bull on the outside and a cow on the inside, both white, like those always seen in the Roman Campagna (fig. 24). Directing the animals counterclockwise, he initiated the *sulcus primigenius*, moving toward the southwest corner of the Palatine. Not far from the Altar of Hercules, he turned left (eastward), and at the bottom of the Stairs of Cacus he raised the ploughshare, probably in anticipation of a gate there, whose name we no longer know. He then continued the furrow toward the southeast corner of the mount, not far from the Altar of Consus, and there he turned left (northward) toward the northeast corner of the eminence, where the building that would house the thirty *curiae* and their communal meals would be built; he turned one last time to the left (westward), raising the ploughshare at the point where the Porta Mugonia was to be built, then lowering it at once, until he was nearly back at his starting point, where he raised the ploughshare again, at the place where the Porta Romanula was to be built (fig. 18). The *pomerium* containing the augury's blessing is thus a continuous boundary, while the *sulcus primigenius* is discontinuous, making provisions for three ritual gates, aside from the side gates. The name of the Porta Romanula—the "little Rome"—testifies to its importance, in that it corresponded to the "supreme" corner from which sprang the *templum in aere* designated to inaugurate the Palatine within the *pomerium*. Following behind Romulus were men who moved aside the dirt clods created on either side of the ploughshare, piling them up on the outside, so that they would represent, in miniature and thus symbolically, the walls and moat. To consolidate the ephemeral furrow and the placement of the gates, three boundary stones—different from those of the *pomerium*, as we have found from our excavation of one part of the wall with a gate that can be identified as the Mugonia (fig. 25)—were laid in the ground. At the Porta Romanula, Romulus sacrificed the bull and cow and addressed a prayer to Jupiter, Mars, and Vesta. These were perhaps the deities originally worshipped at the three gates: Jupiter Stator, in association with the Porta Mugonia; Mars together with Faunus, to whom the Lupercal, in association

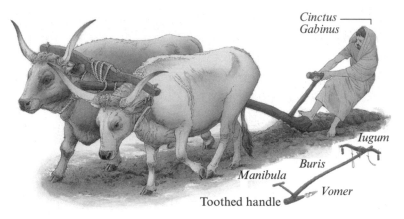

Fig. 24. The king-augur Romulus digs the first furrow (*sulcus primigenius*) with a bronze-bladed plow drawn by a cow and a bull. (Studio Inklink)

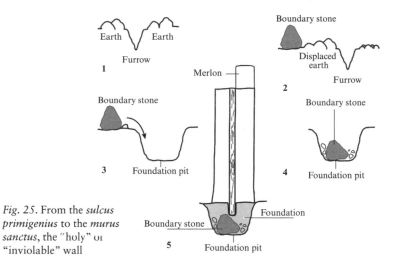

Fig. 25. From the *sulcus primigenius* to the *murus sanctus*, the "holy" or "inviolable" wall

with the gate at the end of the Stairs of Cacus, was sacred; and Vesta together with the Lares, in connection with the Porta Romanula.

The Etruscan ritual envisioned simply a sacred wall (*murus sanctus*)—not an *agger* (bulwark)—whose foundational pit was supposed to be dug by broadening and deepening the *sulcus primigenius*. Into the bottom of this pit—in the stretch we excavated—the men would throw the boundary stones earlier placed along the furrow—nonfigurative images of the god Terminus—thus incorporating them into the walls themselves, confirming the *sanctitas*/inviolability issuing from the quasi-sacralized foundations (fig. 25). Once the walls were completed, a little girl was sacrificed and her attributes buried under the threshold of the Porta Mugonia. The finds of this "foundational deposit"—particularly a cup—are what enabled us to date the completion of the walls to the second quarter of the eighth century BC (figs. 26–28).

This first public works project of Rome, clearly commissioned by a strong, centralized power such as that of the *rex-augur*, represents our first great archaeological discovery, and it has confirmed tradition as concerns Romulus's first achievement. Judging from the location on the Palatium where we found the inscribed cippi commemorating the place in which Remus was believed to have violated the walls and where the founder would be killed—along the so-called Clivus Palatinus ("Palatine Slope") near the Arch of Titus—one would think

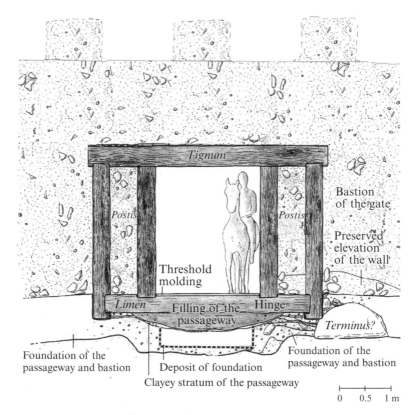

Fig. 26. Reconstruction of a section of the Porta Mugonia of the Romulian walls, Palatine Hill. Internal wooden framework of the gate between two bastions. Under the threshold is the votive foundational deposit.

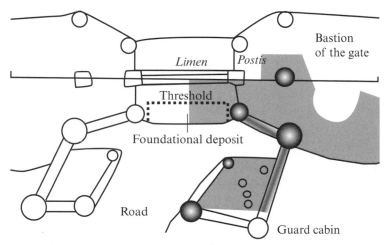

Bastion
of the gate

Limen   *Postis*

Threshold

Foundational deposit

Road

Guard cabin

Fig. 27. Palatine, Romulian walls, Porta Mugonia, plan.

Fig. 28. Palatine, Romulian walls, Porta Mugonia, foundational deposit under the threshold. Funerary attributes of a little girl.

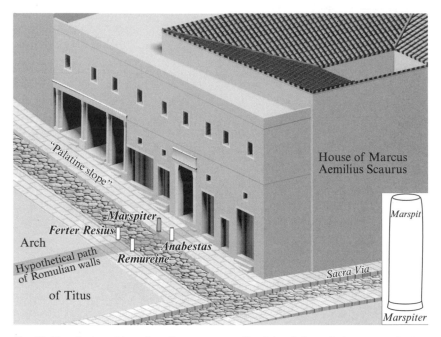

Fig. 29. The cippi marking where Remus supposedly violated the walls (reconstruction).

that the attacker came from the Velia, a hill disparaged and dismissed by Romulus, who excluded it from the *pomerium*, despite the fact that it had been the very ancient seat of the pre-urban community of the Velienses and represented the second mount of the Septimontium (fig. 29). When the walls were later destroyed in order to be rebuilt, around 700 BC, two adults and one small boy would be buried in an enclosure within the razed walls. These might be cases of human sacrifice aimed at expiating the demolition of the first walls, a ritual that appears to reflect the myth of Remus. Whoever violated or moved any boundary stones—and the Palatine walls included stones of this sort—must suffer the condemnation of the *sacer esto*, a curse that cleansed the community of the guilty party and consigned him to the deities of the underworld, to whom he could be offered only through death. Thus did Romulus appear to perform, on this occasion, the first act in defense of the *urbs*, intended to reestablish the *pax deorum*.

THE FOUNDING OF THE FORUM, THE CAPITOL, AND THE CITADEL

※

The Forum

THE SANCTUARY OF VESTA

The place where the Forum was built was, at first, a low-lying valley (six meters below sea level) that often flooded with the waters of the Tiber and was therefore uninhabitable: the Velabrum. The valley lay between the Palatine, the settlement's epicenter, and Mount Saturnius, later called the Capitolium, a stronghold inhabited since circa 1700 BC that had been left out of the great proto-urban center of the Quirites settlement, thus retaining its rural character as an elevated village in a district of the *ager* or *pagus* analogous to the Aventine. One could say that the Quirinal was to the Capitolium what the Palatine was to the Aventine. Descending the Quirinal, the Via Salaria wended its way into this valley at the foot of the Capitolium as far as the ford across the Tiber, beyond which the route continued on, as the Via Campana, toward the Campus Salinarum. At the crucial point, at the edge of the Forum, where the route that would become the Sacra Via intersected the Via Salaria, the Comitium would rise (fig. 30), the place where the *curiae* convened.

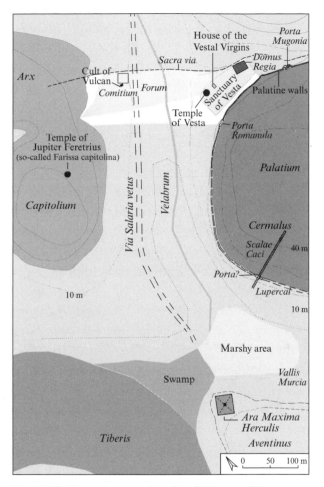

Fig. 30. The Forum between the cults of Vulcan and Vesta.

In order to create a link between the Palatine and the Capitolium, the ground had to be raised at least two meters to form a public square, which would become for Rome what the early archaic agora was for Athens. Just outside the walls of the Palatine—the "forum" was in fact a campus "outside the walls"—and at a prominent point on the slopes of that hill, the Sanctuary of Vesta, an integral part of the Forum complex, was created. This was where the king would descend to live after having left his casa on the Palatine (fig. 20), like Aegeus, who left the Acropolis of Athens for the lower city (*astu*). Within the enclosure of the holy place was a clearing (*lucus*) in which the king's house was grouped with the royal cults of Mars and Ops and the Lares, the house of the vestal virgins, and the communal hearth sacred to Vesta (fig. 31).

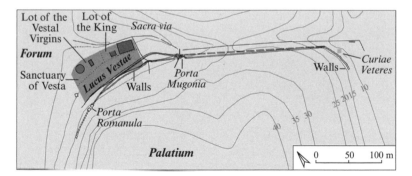

Fig. 31. The Romulian walls: original path and first remaking. Beyond the walls, in the Forum, the Temple of Vesta between the Romanula and Mugonia gates.

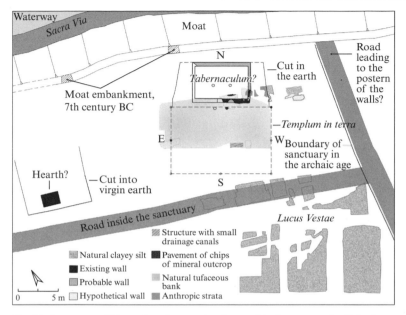

Fig. 32. Sanctuary of Vesta, the tabernaculum/*casa* with observatory for lightning or *templum in terra* (ca. 775/750 BC) and open-air hearths.

AUSPICES FOR CREATING THE SANCTUARY. In the eastern part of the Sanctuary's clearing, just after the walls were built, a small hut was built from remainders of the enclosure in front of it. This was probably a tabernaculum, with an augural *templum* in front, though of a different sort this time because it faced south, as would be necessary for observing not birds but *signa ex caelo*, that is, lightning (figs. 32–33). The purpose of the augury was to obtain divine consent for the establishment, in that place, of the houses of the king and the vestal virgins, the *aedes* of Vesta and, perhaps, the entire Fo-

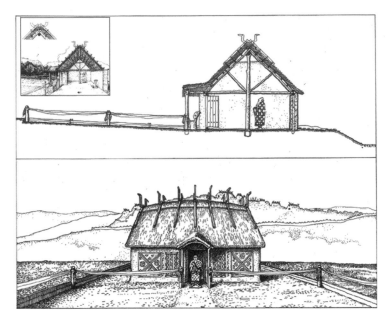

Fig. 33. Sanctuary of Vesta, cross-sections and frontal view of the tabernaculum/ *casa.* (R. Merlo)

rum complex as well. As was the custom before the auguries, it was the founder of the Sanctuary who was to be received in the tabernaculum, so that he could wait for daybreak and for the signs from the sky.

In his *Fasti*, Ovid attributes this event to the last of the founding kings, Numa Pompilius, who, seated on a throne of maple wood—probably in front of his hut—covered his head and prayed until he heard three thunderclaps and observed as many thunderbolts, followed in the end by a shield of un-

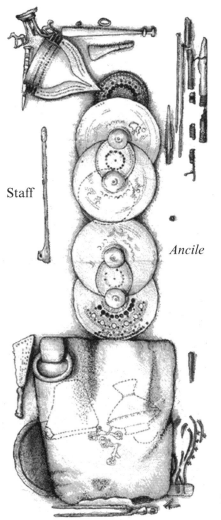

Staff

Ancile

Fig. 34. Veii, Casal Fosso, tomb
1036, 750–725 BC

usual form that fell from the sky, called the *ancile* (fig. 34). The ceremony then ended with a sacrifice. The shield was to be received into the royal dwelling, constructed shortly thereafter, together with eleven other shields that were quickly commissioned so that the original could no longer be identified, it being necessary to protect this supreme talisman of the regnum. When divine consent was obtained, the buildings of the Sanctuary were constructed on ground cleaned to perfection by ploughshares (fig. 49).

The ancients were uncertain whether to attribute the creation of the cult of Vesta to Romulus or to Numa, though they preferred the latter. But in its initial phase, the Sanctuary seems to have been more Romulian than Numan, since it must be dated from around the years 775–750 BC.

THE HOUSE OF THE KING, OR DOMUS REGIA. Immediately following the construction of the hut or tabernaculum, what appears to have been the first *domus* in Rome was built, a small palace constructed still with the same technique as the huts but which had no contemporary equivalents (except, perhaps, at Populonia in Etruria). It must have looked rather like the dwellings of the Roman notables of the time, with which we are, however, unfamiliar. Atop the destroyed tabernaculum, a great room was constructed, with a porch (*prothryon*) supported by two wooden columns and featuring a bench along the walls. This was perhaps the royal sacrarium of Ops and Mars and may have contained the sacred lances and some nonrepresentational images of Mars, as well as the twelve *ancilia* on the walls. The hall must also have housed the royal banquet with its luxurious crockery, some of it of Greek provenance; the guests probably were regaled by the performance of *carmina convivialia*, the subject of which might well have been the saga of the founder (fig. 38). To the sides were the rooms for living and the covered hearth; the thatched roof was supported by poles in front and opened onto a courtyard in back. On the western side of the dwelling was also an open-air fireplace. The spot would later be occupied by the *aedes Larum*, and thus it is possible that subsequent early-archaic hearths were already sacred to the Lares. A little girl would be sacrificed and buried, along with her attributes, in a corner of the courtyard, and serve as the "foundational deposit"; the rite—already known from its practice at the gates in the wall—would be repeated in the Domus at least two more times.

It is the ceramics contained in these deposits of attributes that enable us to date the building, a structure still based on the same techniques as the huts but one that anticipated planimetric designs that later became known in Etruria (figs. 35–36). The Domus would later undergo a variety of adaptations and reconstructions; there is evidence of four phases over one and a half centuries. First the building was expanded to one side to form an L, to make a second hall available—possibly the sacrarium, henceforth separate from the banquet hall (fig. 37). It was later enlarged and finally endowed with walls with tufa chips at the base and a tiled roof. In this last phase, which dates from the second half of the seventh century BC, the building's construction technique surpassed that used for the huts and featured a more structured open-air hearth. The last human sacrifice known to us dates from the

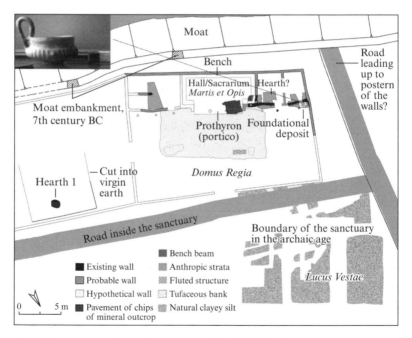

Fig. 35. Sanctuary of Vesta, Domus Regia, 750–725 BC. *Upper left*, the dipping cup found in the funerary attributes of a little girl buried in the "foundation deposit" of the house.

end of this house's existence, around 600 BC, and functioned as an "obliteration deposit" (fig. 39). The dwelling's different phases spanned the entire first royal era, representing the home of the kings of Rome until Tarquinius Priscus. Literary sources, when properly interpreted, associate the houses of Numa and Ancus Marcius with the Sanctuary of Vesta, and Vesta herself with the cult of the Lares. They assign a dwelling to Tullus Hostilius on the Velia, but this must have been

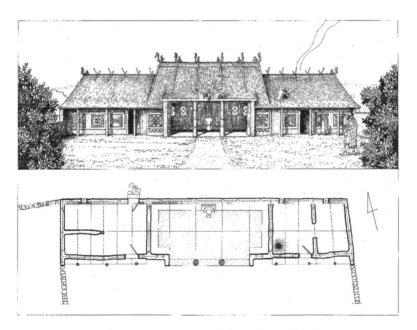

Fig. 36. Sanctuary of Vesta, reconstruction of frontal view of the Domus Regia. (R. Merlo)

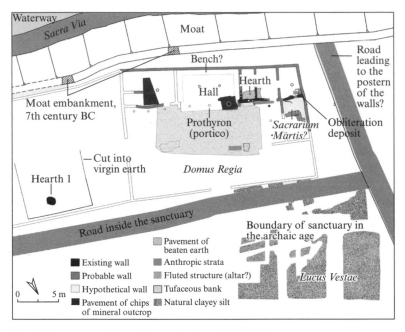

Fig. 37. Sanctuary of Vesta, Domus Regia, ca. 725–700 BC.

this king's royal residence, as it was elevated and thus more easily defended, and not the sovereign's official seat, which was presumably still in the Sanctuary. Only a king-augur, as described in the *constitutio Romuli* and exercising *patria potestas* over the vestal virgins, could be allowed to live in the Forum's Sanctuary. This ensemble of finds represents our second great archaeological discovery.

Fig. 38. Sanctuary of Vesta, reconstruction of the banquet hall/sacrarium with the lances of Mars and the *ancilia* against the walls.

THE SANCTUARY IN THE AGE OF THE TARQUINI (LATE SEVENTH CENTURY TO LATE SIXTH CENTURY BC). Under the Tarquini and Servius Tullius, the Sanctuary was entirely restructured (fig. 40), indicating a great historical turning point. A second *domus regia* was built between the eastern boundary of the Sanctuary and the Porta Mugonia in its fourth century BC version. This large dwelling was connected to the Lucus Vestae by a highly significant passageway that

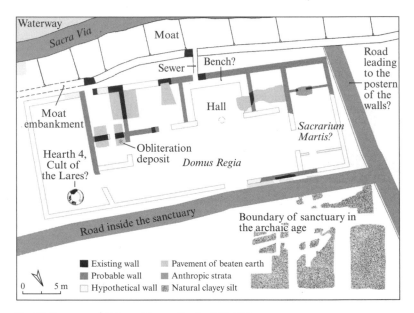

Fig. 39. Sanctuary of Vesta, Domus Regia, 650–600 BC.

makes it possible to identify the structure as the house of the Tarquini, since only the sovereign was allowed to communicate directly with the vestal virgins. Literary sources speak of a *domus* of the two Tarquini, which we can probably interpret as a building in several phases at a single site, a house that a close, critical reading situates within the Vesta complex. And this is our third great archaeological discovery. The new

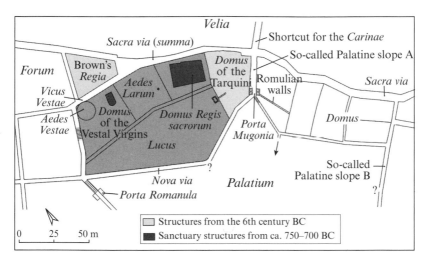

Fig. 40. The early-archaic and archaic Sanctuary of Vesta.

dwelling outside the Sanctuary is an important indication of a more secular, tyrannical royalty that has its justification in the provisions of Tarquinius Priscus and in the constitutional reform of Servius Tullius. With the advent of the Republic, this second *domus regia* would become *domus publica*, the residence of the *pontifex maximus* containing the city's most important archive (fig. 41); on the other hand, the same *pontifex maximus* could have been a priestly office created at the time of the Tarquini, which later, with the Republic, became the high priest of the State.

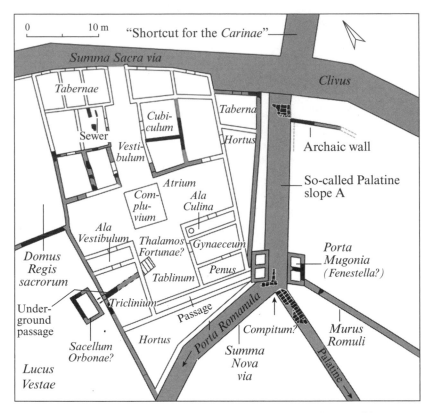

Fig. 41. Reconstruction of the *domus* of the Tarquini, later the *domus publica,* between the Sanctuary of Vesta and the Porta Mugonia, with a passage from the *tablinum* to the Lucus Vestae.

The old Domus Regia within the Sanctuary was not, however, abandoned; it was restructured, its layout transformed (fig. 42). Who could have lived in it, given that only the vestal virgins and a man of royal rank could inhabit the sacred enclosure? It was probably a second king created by the Tarquini: the king of sacrifices (*rex sacrorum*)—that is, the

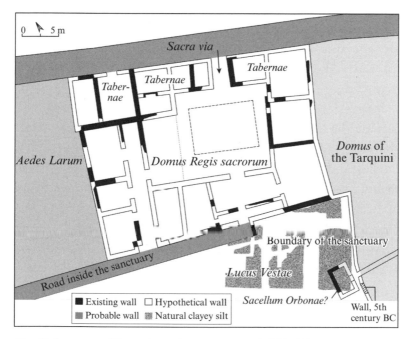

Fig. 42. Sanctuary of Vesta, *domus Regis sacrorum*, 550/53–500 BC.

ancient king-augur reduced to solely sacrificial functions, all the political and military powers having transferred to *reges-magistri* of a tyrannical character living nearby, just outside the Sanctuary. Contemporary historians are uncertain as to whether to attribute the creation of the king of sacrifices to the Tarquinian era or to the first Republic; the archaeology confirms the former hypothesis. And this was our fourth great archaeological discovery.

At the time of the Tarquini, the cults of Mars and Ops, already admitted in the more ancient Domus Regia, were not transferred into the dwelling of these kings, nor were they left in the house that was, by that point, occupied by the king of sacrifices. At that time, a sacrarium was built for them just outside the Sanctuary, beyond the Vicus Vestae—known archaeologically as the Regia unearthed by F. Brown—in which the lances of the god Mars and the *ancilia* were kept. This is another indication of the secularized character of the tyrants of Rome, who freed their official residence from the sacred restraints of the first royal age.

At the center of the Sanctuary, between the plot of the king of sacrifices and that of the vestal virgins, an intermediate plot was created, now housing a silo and probably a first edifice or *aedes*, built over the open-air hearths of the more ancient royal domicile (fig. 43): likely the first *aedes Larum*—the cult of the Lares now being certainly public—separate from that

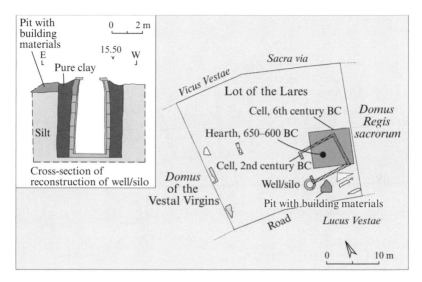

Fig. 43. Sanctuary of Vesta, *aedes Larum*, reconstruction of the sixth-century BC cell, with well/silo.

of the Lar Familiaris of Tarquinius Priscus, mystical father of Servius Tullius; from that of Mars and Ops; and from that of Vesta. Between the second century BC and the time of Augustus, the *aedes Larum* would become a monumental complex endowed with cells, a porticoed courtyard, and underground lararium (fig. 44). Augustus would later consign his Lares and his Genius to the vestal virgins—the scene is represented on the Ara Belvedere, or Belvedere Altar—and they would thereafter become the Lares of the city's quarters, just as those of

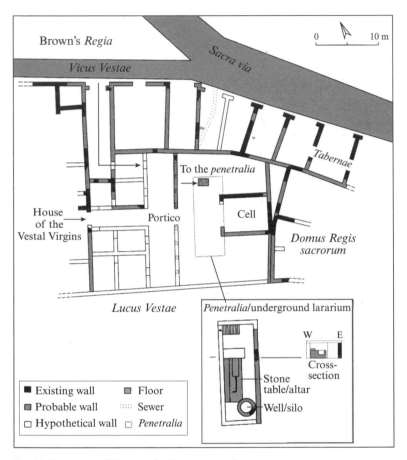

Fig. 44. Sanctuary of Vesta, *aedes Larum*, second century BC

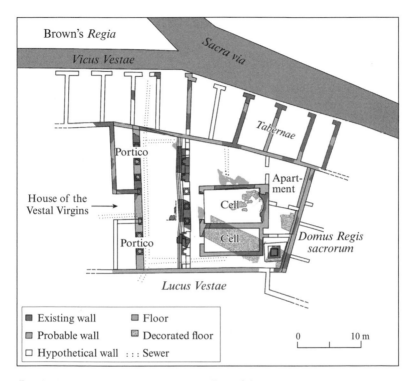

Fig. 45. Sanctuary of Vesta, a*edes Larum,* Second Augustan Age.

Servius Tullius and, even earlier, those of Romulus, had been. Now, alongside the cell of the public Lares was a smaller cell, probably designed to receive the Lares of Augustus (perhaps along with his testament and exploits?) (figs. 45–46). And this was our fifth great archaeological discovery.

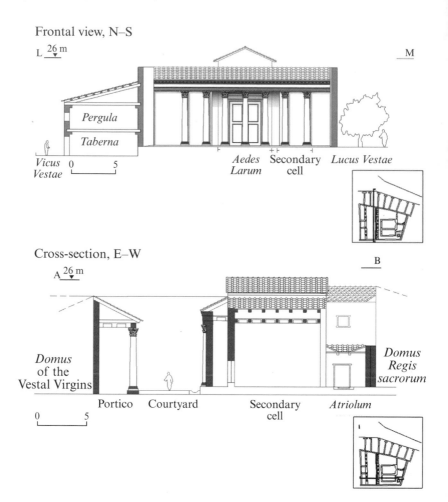

Frontal view, N–S

L 26 m

M

Pergula

Taberna

Vicus 0 5
Vestae

Aedes   Secondary   Lucus Vestae
Larum   cell

Cross-section, E–W

A 26 m

B

Domus
of the
Vestal Virgins

Domus
Regis
sacrorum

Portico   Courtyard   Secondary   Atriolum
cell

0 5

Fig. 46. Sanctuary of Vesta, reconstruction of the *aedes Larum*, second Augustan age.

With Nero's great fire (AD 64) and the creation of the Clivus Sacer (lit., "Holy Slope"), which connected the surviving Regia with the central core of the Domus Aurea, only the *aedes Vestae* was saved. The rest of the Sanctuary complex was buried under the vast portico of the Clivus, and a huge new house of the vestal virgins was built farther uphill. One part of Augustus's *domus*, built on the Cermalus in front of the Casa Romuli, would be the new *domus publica* of the *princeps pontifex maximus*. The house of the king of sacrifices and the *aedes Larum* would be demolished. We don't know whether the king of sacrifices was subsequently lodged in an apartment of the new house of the vestals.

THE HOUSE OF THE VESTAL VIRGINS AND THE AEDES VESTAE. We know little about the primitive *aedes Vestae* and would probably find little more by excavation—perhaps a few horizontal strata outside of the *aedes*? This edifice must originally have been a round hut, situated where the *aedes* of the Imperial Era now stands, whose foundation in Roman concrete (*opus caementicium*)—combined with archaeological excavations—have destroyed all preexisting structures. But the foundation itself reveals a rectangular *penus* at the center of the rotunda, in which a number of talismans, including a mysterious phallus, were supposed to have been.

We have succeeded in acquainting ourselves with the *domus*, in its various parts, of the vestals of the First Empire and

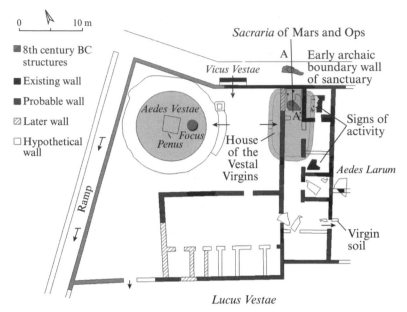

Fig. 47. Sanctuary of Vesta, Late-Republican house of the vestal virgins. Underneath are the hut of the vestal virgins (770–725 BC), in front of the *aedes Vestae*, and the boundary wall of the Sanctuary.

the late Republic and, to a lesser degree, with the *domus* of the archaic era (fig. 47). But the greater discovery, the sixth made in our excavations, concerned the primitive hut of the vestal virgins unearthed from below the archaic dwelling, probably rectangular in form. Its door must have been situated in front of that of the primitive *aedes Vestae*, so that the vestal virgins, by passing through it, could attend to the sacred fire, which was supposed to burn perpetually in the hearth of Vesta and be renewed every first day of March. Beside the hut, the first walls enclosing the Sanctuary were unearthed, as well as the first flooring of the Vicus Vestae (fig. 48)—discoveries datable, thanks to a fragment of Euboean crockery, to the second quarter of the eighth century BC and after. Beneath these constructions, the soil of the mid-eighth century BC finally appeared, presenting traces of tilling performed with a ploughshare and probably connected with the deforestation and clearing that preceded the construction of the Sanctuary (fig. 49).

SYNTHESIS. We can conclude that Romulus's first achievement, involving the blessing and walling of the Palatine, dates from the second quarter of the eighth century BC, and a fun-

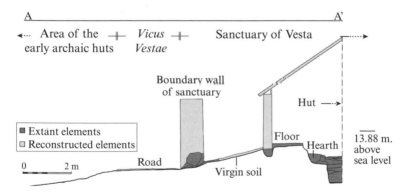

Fig. 48. Sanctuary of Vesta, the boundary wall of the Sanctuary and the hut of the vestal virgins, 770–725 BC.

Fig. 49. Sanctuary of Vesta, humus with traces of plowing predating the Sanctuary of Vesta.

damental part of the second achievement, involving the Sanctuary of Vesta in the Forum, also dates from the same part of the century, which would make it part of the same project of Romulus. We therefore have not only the *urbs* on the Palatine but also the sacred and political center of the regnum. We have, moreover, as we shall see, the civic cult of Jupiter Feretrius on the Capitolium and the definitive *templum* of augury, or Auguraculum, of the Roman state—perhaps in association with the cult of Juno?—situated on the Arx. Lastly we have, from its very beginnings, the city but also the state. Historians who have admitted the existence of only the city by the mid-eighth century have tried to postdate at least the political and state dimension, but their version does not take into account the data from the new excavations, and indeed conflicts with it, and must therefore be discarded.

THE FORUM AS PUBLIC SQUARE

Atop an earlier stratum of filling, two meters thick and datable to the second half of the eighth century BC, we unearthed the first pebbled pavement of the Forum, datable to the last quarter of that century or, at the latest, the first quarter of the following century (fig. 50). The project of reclamation, elevation, and preparation was clearly begun in the Romulian era—as tradition has it—and finished in the Numan era. The age of Tullus Hostilius added only improvements to the original project, which should be considered as having been completed at the time of the founding kings. What was once erroneously considered to be the first pavement of the Forum, created on top of a second filling of the valley, is actually the second paving of the square and can be dated around the mid-seventh century BC. This error was the basis on which the late dating of the Forum was made. A new examination of the square, including an excavation of its southern end under the Curia Julia, and another of the Comitium (whose covering is now decaying and needs to be redone) are imperative.

THE SANCTUARY OF VULCAN AND THE COMITIUM

Just as the royal abode was admitted within the Sanctuary of Vesta, so the royal council, which included the notables of Rome, was contained within the Sanctuary of Vulcan, or Volcanal. Both places were slightly higher than the Forum

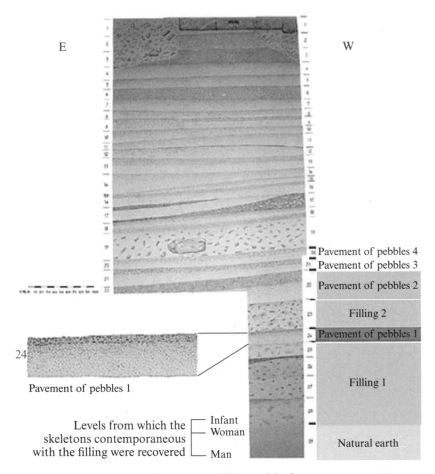

E

W

Pavement of pebbles 4
Pavement of pebbles 3
Pavement of pebbles 2

Filling 2

Pavement of pebbles 1

Filling 1

Pavement of pebbles 1

24

Natural earth

Levels from which the skeletons contemporaneous with the filling were recovered

— Infant
— Woman
— Man

Fig. 50. The Forum with the first stratum of filling and the first pavement, ca. 700 BC (for placement, cf. fig. 51).

square and constituted its boundaries along the shorter sides (fig. 30). Unfortunately—as we saw with the *aedes Vestae*—the ancient modifications of the Volcanal, and the antiquated form of excavation used, have made the archaeological reconstruction of the site an arduous task. The fact remains that the most ancient votive finds associated with the Volcanal date from the late eighth century BC. Also from the same era are the two strata spared by the *cavea*-shaped Comitium of Tullus Hostilius. Given the nature of the site, these strata can be ascribed not to habitational structures but to the primitive Comitium (fig. 51). What, after all, would a city-state

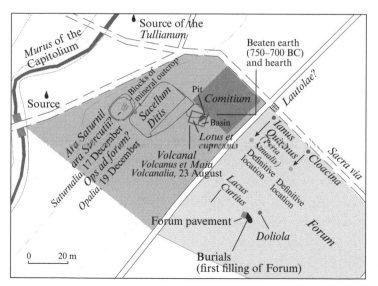

Fig. 51. The Forum with the Sanctuary of Vulcan and the Comitium (reconstruction).

and kingdom be without a place in which to convene the *curiae*, something analogous to where the *curiae* met to share their meals? Tradition attributes the creation of the Forum and the Comitium to Romulus and Titus Tatius, who supposedly formed an alliance and a double monarchy in the very place where the Comitium would later stand—in which case, Titus Tatius, too, was made king of Rome, legitimated, and inaugurated (perhaps on the Arx?).

Finally, Romulus was supposedly killed and quartered by the royal counselors in the selfsame Volcanal, the existence of which is therefore taken for granted in the myth of death. The royal coronation of Numa likewise presupposes the existence of a discretionary Comitium and an augural *templum* on the Arx. Despite the absence of proper excavations at these sites, the archaeology on the whole confirms tradition, even concerning these institutions and their public headquarters. The Romulian constitution handed down to us by Cicero and Dionysius of Halicarnassus indeed provides for a king-augur with an official seat within the Sanctuary of Vesta (as we know from the scholars of ancient Rome), a royal council first in the Volcanal and later in the Curia Hostilia, and people's assemblies at the Comitium next to the Volcanal (*comitia curiata*) and on the Capitolium in front of the Curia Calabra (*comitia calata*). These were the political bodies provided for in the original dispensation, and in conjunction with the high priests of the state, they counterbalanced the power of the king-augur, who thus appears as a prototype of the constitutional monarch. Linking the Comitium with the house of the king was the Sacra Via—that is, the most important stretch of this street, which passes through the Forum and is therefore public—along which the king would escape (from politics) once a year and retreat into his own house, in the mysterious rite known as the Regifugium, attributable in the Romulian calendar to December 24.

The Capitolium and the Arx

On the Capitolium, just outside the base on which the enormous Temple of Jupiter Optimus Maximus would later rest, stood the first temple of the civic cult of Rome, consecrated by Romulus to Jupiter Feretrius. The worship of Jupiter King of the Tarquini, was thus the city's second civic cult. This first temple probably included a sacred enclosure within which we can imagine an *aedes*, originally a hut, with an altar in front of it. The enclosure was supposedly created in front of a sacred oak, from which Romulus is said to have hung the mortal remains of Acron, the rebellious lord of Caenina (fig. 59), as a bloody example of a crushed revolt (figs. 52–53) after defeating and killing him. The first triumphal procession (*ovatio*), led by the king, on foot, carrying Acron's mortal remains, began at the bottom of the Velia Hill, at the Lucus Streniae,

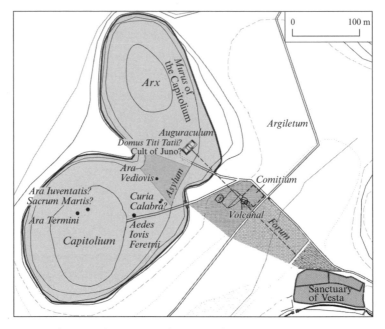

Fig. 52. The Capitolium, Arx, and Forum and its sanctuaries.

and had as its destination none other than the Temple of Jupiter Feretrius. The military procession of the *ovatio*, along the Sacra Via, thus took place outside the Palatine *pomerium*, due to the sacred interdiction against contaminating the *urbs* with the presence of men-at-arms.

The nonrepresentational image (*signum*) of Feretrius was a semiprecious stone, the lapis silex, probably a prehistoric axe (fig. 54) thought to be a *keraunos*—that is, the materializa-

Fig. 53. The Capitolium, sacred oak, *templum*, and hut of Jupiter Feretrius.
(Studio Inklink)

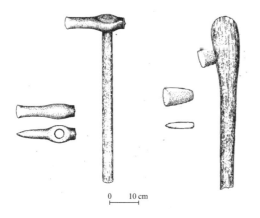

Fig. 54. Stone axes used
to rebuild the *signum* of
Jupiter Feretrius.

0   10 cm

tion of a lightning bolt (as in the case of another talisman-weapon, the *ancile*). Indeed the stone, when struck, would emit sparks. One of the first manifestations of the *ius* was the *ius iurandum*, or oath. In taking the oath, the priest would brandish this lapis to sacrifice a sow. Anyone violating the oath would meet a similar end, struck down by Jupiter. Thus to the civil and military aspect of the cult was now added a juridical one, which should be seen in this case as the divine and human apparatus underlying the identity of the Romans, whose earthly representative was the king-augur.

A deposit unearthed, along with a few structures, on the Capitoline, under the Protomoteca and associated, correctly, with the Temple of Feretrius, contains votive artifacts dating from the second half of the eighth century BC and thereafter (fig. 55), providing an invaluable clue to establishing the origin of the cult.

From the beginning, at the site where the Temple of Tarquinian Jupiter would later rise, the nonrepresentational image of Terminus was displayed for worship: a large stone marking the vertex of the *ager* (the Capitolium originally had an analogous pagan statue on the Aventine). A similar, corresponding stone marked the boundary of the *ager* in the *oppidum* at Acqua Acetosa Laurentina (fig. 59). The feast of the Terminalia, held on December 23 in the ten-month Romulian calendar, must therefore have involved the center as well as the periphery of the regnum. Once the Arx/Citadel

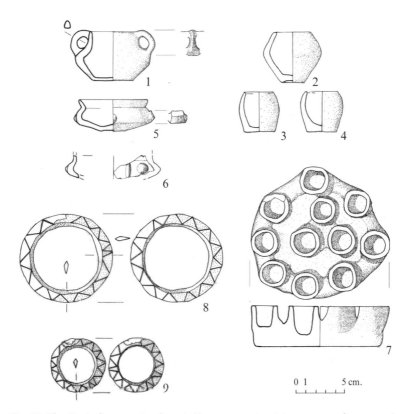

Fig. 55. The Capitolium, votive deposit (Protomoteca): miniature vases, *kernos*, and bronze rings, second half of eighth century BC. (E. Gusberti)

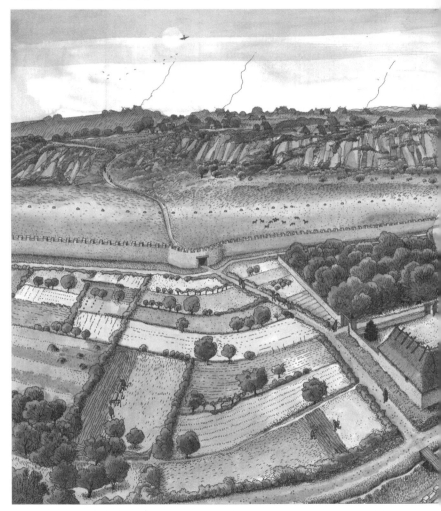

Fig. 56. Reconstruction of the urban landscape of early Rome. *Lower right*, the Velia with the Murus Mustellinus; *center*, the Sacra Via with the Sanctuary of Vesta; *foreground*, the Domus Regia (cf. fig. 37); *at the back*, the hut of the Vestal Virgins

(cf. figs. 47 and 48) and the *aedes Vestae* with the *lucus* behind it; *background*, the Palatine and its walls; *upper right*, the Forum, under preparation, and the Capitolium. (R. Merlo)

was established at the top of the Capitolium closest to the Quirinal—an external yet essential complement of the *urbs*—the definitive augural observatory of Rome, later associated with the cult of Juno, was established there, having perhaps had early-archaic antecedents, since, dating back to the most ancient calendars, the couple of Jupiter and Juno had been worshipped at the start and the middle of the month. The goddess thus ended up playing a fundamental theological, indeed structural, role alongside that of the triad composed of Jupiter, Mars, and Quirinus.

A reconstruction of the urban landscape between the Velia, Palatine, Forum, and Capitolium (fig. 56), gives us an idea of the heart of the original city (that is, of the first and second achievements).

THE ORDERING OF THE REGNUM,
OR THE *CONSTITUTIO ROMULI*

——— ✿ ———

The Ordering of Time

Tradition has it that Rome's first calendar had ten months. Some time ago, Mommsen noticed that the epigraphs conveying the city's calendar display certain feast days in larger characters. These dates are the solid core, always present, and should, according to Mommsen, be attributed to the original calendar. A variety of literary sources, moreover, maintain that the Romulian year lasted ten months, like human pregnancy. While numerous historians consider this information a fairy tale, Italy's greatest historian of religions, Angelo Brelich, is not among them. Encouraged by his study of ancient calendars, I tried to reconstruct the Romulian calendar, alternating months of thirty and twenty-nine days—indeed, the aversion to even-numbered days comes after the early archaic age. It is interesting to note that our own last month of the year, December, refers to the number ten—*dix*—whereby we may surmise that the year must have begun in March. Indeed the oldest known Roman New Year's date was March 15. At first I could not determine why the year ended on December 23, the feast of the Terminalia. One can understand a beginning at the start or the middle of a month, but why the twenty-third for the end? Recalling that the ancients held that the human pregnancy lasted 274 days, I began counting the days starting from March 15 to the dawn of December 24, and I noticed that the sum comes to exactly 274 (fig. 57). From this I deduced that the end of the symbolic human pregnancy, and thus the *dies natalis* of the Romans, fell on the dawn of December 24. The birthday of Christ attested to from the fourth century AD would fall only one day later, on the twenty-fifth of the same month. Between the end of the year on December 23 and the beginning of the new year on March 15 fell a period characterized by barrenness. Indeed, before the start of menstruation and in the days following childbirth, a woman is sterile.

The calendar was created by the king at the start of each month, in front of the Curia Calabra on the Capitolium, a place from which, by observing the sky, the feast days were governed according to the movements of the moon.

The Ordering of Space and Men

All the literary sources recount that the soil and men of the Roman *ager* were divided into three tribes (*tribus*), a partition probably of proto-urban origin: note the divisibility by three of the twenty-seven sacraria of the Argei, the pre-civic cults located in the settlement's various neighborhoods (*curiae*), which didn't yet conform to the Romulian decimal system. Only with the founding of the city does the number of *curiae* come to thirty, also a number divisible by three; but the number of Argei remains sacredly frozen at twenty-seven (fig. 58). One might infer that the tribes coincided with the pre-urban districts of three *populi Albenses* attested near the ford in the Tiber (fig. 4). The tribe of Titienses, between the Tiber and the Via Prenestina, would thus coincide with the Latinienses, who had their fortress on the Collis Latiaris; the tribe of the Ramnes, between the Via Prenestina and the Via Appia, would coincide with the Querquetulani, who had their fortress on the Querquetal/Caelius; the tribe of the Luceres, between the Via Appia and the Tiber, would coincide with the district of the Velienses, who had their fortress on the Velia (figs. 59 and 6).

The *tribus* had their origin between the Subura foothill, the Subura mountain, the Corneta at the foot of the Velia, and the Argiletum at the foot of the Arx, where the Porticus Absidata—also a nerve center for subsequent regional subdivision—would later stand, and extended as far as the limits of the *ager*. The *ager*—the countryside surrounding the settlement—was subdivided not only into the large tribal slices but also concentrically. The majority of the lots of the individual citizens, measuring two *iugera* (one-half hectare) in size, must have been situated between the built-up settlement and the first mile, which was marked by sanctuaries (fig. 59), while

	MARTIVS	APRILIS	MAIVS	IVNIUS	QVINCTILIS
	I	II	III	IV	V

	MARTIVS	APRILIS	MAIVS	IVNIUS	QVINCTILIS
13			LEMVRIA Lemuribus.		
14	EQVIRRIA Marti Mamuralia (?).				
15	EID. Feriae Iovi; Annae Perennae. **1**	EID. Feriae Iovi; FORDICIDIA Telluri Marti.	EID. Feriae Iovi; itur ad Argeos	EID. Feriae Iovi; Vesta clauditur; Q.ST.D.F. (Quando stercus delatum, fas).	EID. Feriae Iovi.
16	Itur ad Argeos.				
17	LIBERALIA Libero, Liberae; AGONALIA Martia; itur ad Argeos.		Ambarvalia Deae Diae (?).		
18	.				
19	QVINQVATRVS Marti; ancilia moventur, saltatio saliorum in Comitio	CERIALIA Cereri.			LVCARIA.
20					
21		PARILIA Pali; Roma condita.	AGONALIA Vediovi (?).		LVCARIA.
22					
23	TUBILVSTRIUM Marti, ancilia moventur.	VINALIA (priora) Iovi.	TUBILVSTRIUM Volcano.		NEPTUNALIA Neptuno.
24	Q.R.C.F. (Quando Rex comitavit, fas).		Q.R.C.F. (Quando Rex comitavit, fas).		
25		ROBIGALIA Robigo.			FVRRINALIA Furrinae.
26					
27				Laribus (?); Iovi Statori (?).	
28					
29		***		***	
30	***		***		***

1 New Year's Day (*Anna Perenna*) ▢ 274 days of pregnancy
▢ 21 days of barrenness 274 Day of birth, year's end (*Terminalia*)

	SEXTILIS II = SEPTEMBER	SEPTEMBER II = NOVEMBER			
	SEXTILIS I = SEXTILIS	SEPTEMBER I= OCTOBER	OCTOBER = DECEMBER	NOVEMBER = IANUARIUS	DECEMBER = FEBRUARIUS
	VI	VII	VIII	IX	X
13			FONTINALIA Fonti.			Parentalia.
14					
15	EID. Feriae Iovi.	EID. Feriae Iovi; Iovi Feretrio (?); (September=) October equus Marti (?).	EID. Feriae Iovi; CONSUALIA Conso.	EID. Feriae Iovi; CARMENTALIA Carmenta.	EID. Feriae Iovi. LVPERCALIA Fauno Luperco.
16					
17	PORTVNALIA Portuno.		SATVRNALIA Saturno.		QVIRNALIA Quirino.
18					
19	VINALIA (rustica vel altera Iovi)	ARMILVSTRIVM Marti, ancilia moventur.	OPALIA Opi ad Forum.		
20					
21	CONSUALIA Conso.		DIVALIA Angeronae.		FERALIA dis inferis, Tacitae Mutae.
22					
23	VOLCANALIA Volcano, Horae Quirini, Maiae supra Comitium		LARENTALIA Accae Larentinae Iovi.		TERMINALIA Termino. 274
24					REGIFVGIVM Iovi?.
25	OPICONSIVA Opi Consiviae in regia.				
26					
27	VOLTVRNALIA Volturo.				EQVIRRIA Marti.
28					
29	***		***		***
30		***		***	

Fig. 57. The Romulian year of ten months, which comprises 274 days (equal to the duration of human pregnancy), and the twenty-one days that fall between the end of the year and new year's day, which symbolize a period of barrenness.

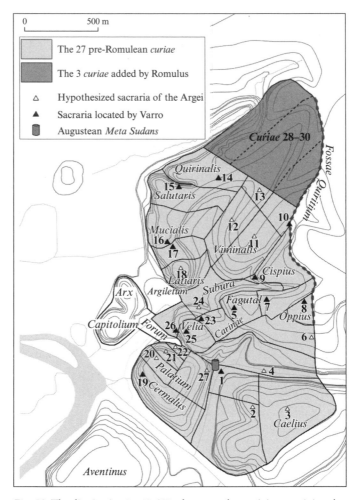

Fig. 58. The districts/*curiae* (1–27) of proto-urban origin containing the sacraria of the Argei, and the three curiae (28–30) added by Romulus.

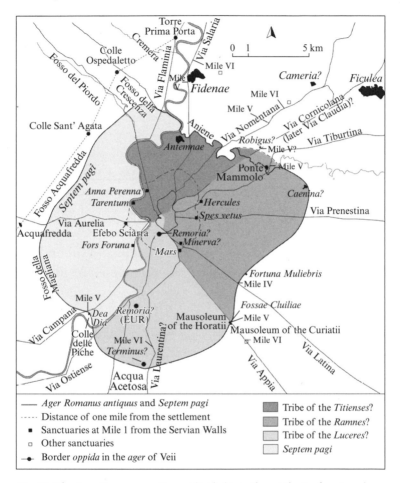

Fig. 59. The Ager Romanus antiquus (divided into three tribes), of proto-urban origin, and the Septem Pagi, conquered by Romulus.

between the first mile and the limit of the *ager* lay the lands controlled by the *gentes* and tilled by the *clientes*. The tribes of the settlement were broken up into quarters or *montes/ colles*, into *curiae*, and beyond the settled area, into rural districts or *pagi*. The auxiliary *tribus* of the king, called *tribuni militum*, were in charge.

In the light of a recent study by L. Capogrossi Colognesi,[1] we have calculated that the settlement plus the *ager* (starting perhaps at the Fossae Quiritium?) up to the first mile might contain 3,680 Romulian lots of two *iugera* each (480 of them in the settlement and 3,200 in the *ager*, if we include Trastevere). Of these, 3,300 were supposed to be assigned to young men-at-arms, some with living fathers (380) and thus not entitled to own property (*alieno iuri subjecti*), and many more (2,920) who were already *patres familias* and therefore entitled to own property (*sui iuris*). There were supposed to have been 380 elderly *patres familias* entitled to property, proprietors of their own estates and those of their adult male offspring. We can therefore reconstruct, in theory, a community made up of 6,600 young people, half of them male and half of them female (equal to roughly 37 percent of the population); children small and large, male and female, must have numbered 8,918.9 (equal to roughly 50 percent); the elderly must have numbered 2,318.9 (equal to roughly 13 percent), of which 1,159.4 were male, if they had lived into

---

[1] "Curie, centurie e 'heredia,'" in *Studi in onore di Francesco Grelle* (Bari: Edipuglia, 2006), pp. 41–49.

old age—however, given the high mortality rate in that era, it would be more conservative to assume only a small number of these as still alive—roughly one-third, or 380 individuals. The whole community of Quirites must thus have numbered some 17,837.8 souls, roughly speaking. The 100 *patres familias* of the royal council must therefore have represented an elite of less than one-fourth of the *patres sui iuris*.

Divided into three tribes, the Quirites' settlement was broken up into *montes* and *colles* and, more minutely into thirty *curiae*, twenty-seven of which can be reconstructed thanks to the positions of certain sacraria of the Argei handed down to us by Varro. This does not imply that the Argei were *pro curiis* cults, since they were in fact defined as *pro sacellis* cults, which were nevertheless, by force of circumstance, accepted into the *curiae* (fig. 58). If Quirinus is a deity from the polytheism of the site of Rome and probably existed before the founding of the city; if there were twenty-seven proto-urban *curiae*—as many as the Argei—(defended perhaps by the Fossae Quiritium?); and if, in the formula of the Romans' *res publica*—*populus Romanus Quiritesque*—the Quirites seem a more ancient element than the *populus Romanus*; then the Romani constitute the new element that make the difference with the past. The *curiae* would convene centrally in the *comitia curiata*, and their *iuvenes* formed the organized army, mirroring these *comitia*. In this citizens' army, the 3,000 foot soldiers were supplemented by three inaugurated *centuriae*, which likely formed the king's bodyguard in peacetime: these were the 300 *celeres* commanded by three *tribuni celerum*.

The *constitutio Romuli* described by Cicero and Dionysius regulated royal sovereignty and the secondary powers of the other instituted bodies of the *civitas*. The king-augur and *in(du)perator* (Ennius), who had auxiliaries and a mounted guard, was *potentissimus* both with respect to the priestly order—composed of the *flamines* of the divine triad and the five *pontifices*, in addition to the vestal virgins—and with respect to the Quirites gathered in the *comitia calata* and *curiata*, where the king "stated" his *ius*, and from which bodies his army was formed. Priests, royal council, and *comitia* were collegial assemblies that counterbalanced royal power, which thus was not absolute. Mommsen defined this order as a constitutional monarchy.

Enemies

INTERNAL ENEMIES WITHIN THE AGER

Both Remus and Romulus must have belonged to the mountain *tribus* of the Luceres—in its early, proto-urban phase—since they had been raised on the Cermalus Hill. Remus wanted to found his *oppidum* in the *ager*, on the Aventine or somewhere not much farther, probably in the area where the EUR district now stands (fig. 59). Both of these places must have formed part of the *ager* of Remus, the Remorinus. Romulus instead wished to found an *urbs* in the heart of the proto-urban mountain settlement, on the Cermalus/Palatium (fig. 18), leaving out the already noble Velia. Coming from the Velia declassed by Romulus, Remus violated the sacred walls of the Roma Quadrata (fig, 29)—where the Arch of Titus would one day stand—and was killed by Romulus as an "internal enemy," inasmuch as he belonged to the same tribe and was closely involved in the exploit of the founding, which justifies his appearance—in legend—as the founder's twin brother. (During the initiation, Remus was the successful leader of his age group, but after the first auspices and auguries, Romulus came to prevail.) With Remus dead, the *tribus* of the Luceres was henceforth controlled by Romulus and dominated from the inaugurated, walled Palatine, which served as a royal citadel.

Next, Romulus confronted Acron, petty king of Caenina (La Rustica), an outlying *oppidum* of the Ramnes tribe, whose base in the settlement must have been located on the Esquiline Hill (between the Cispius, Fagutal/Oppius, and Celius). The founder defeated and killed the rebellious lord, who had gone over to the Sabines, and, in front of Acron's mortal remains, which he had hung from a sacred oak on the Capitolium, he instituted the civic cult of Jupiter Feretrius as a warning to discourage all nobility from revolting against the king's power.

Finally, Romulus confronted the enemies from the more troublesome, distant *tribus* of the Titienses said to be in the *colles*. He defeated the rebellion of the Antemnae (modern-day Forte Antenne), whose leaders are unknown to us, but he did not overcome Tarpeius, the lord of the future Capitoline Arx-Citadel. Also a collaborator with the Sabines, Tarpeius, together with his daughter, Tarpeia, opened up this *oppidum* on the periphery of the hill settlement to King Titus Tatius of Cures, who took over that eminence and built his home there (and perhaps also his augural temple). Both father and daughter would eventually be killed by Tatius and Romulus, but the Arx-Citadel remained in Sabine hands. With the Romans unable to defeat the Sabines in the valley that would become the Forum, and with the Sabines equally unable to prevail, the conflict eventually ended with an alliance, and a compromise was arranged whereby Titus Tatius would reign alongside Romulus.

The second phase of early Rome's creation was thus realized jointly by the two kings. Rome, in this light, appears as the final outcome of an interethnic, Latin-Sabine initiative by the ford in the Tiber. Instances of internal resistance to Romulus's undertaking—which, as we have seen, were widespread throughout the territory—give a sense of how innovative and bloody this founding and creation of a city-state must have been.

LATIN AND ETRUSCAN ENEMIES

If we compare the settlement of the Roman site to that of Veii, we note that the first was bigger than the second. But if we compare the two territories, we see the opposite: the original Roman *ager* is only one-fifth the size of Veii's, too small for so considerable a settlement that was larger than any of the Etruscan cities (fig. 9). That the proto-urban center that predated Rome showed signs of weakness can be gathered from this territorial inferiority, among other things. Hence the need for the first two kings—originating from the pre-urban villages of Alba and Cures and backed by their bands—to defeat, one by one, the rebellions of the "barons" of the Septimontium and make them subject to a centralized sovereignty. Their authority was royal at the urban level as well as foreign and thus *super partes*, in the sense that it could not be granted to the nobles of the area, it reflected different ethnic interests on the left bank of the Tiber, and it entailed a balancing of sovereignty itself through the bifurcation of royalty and the secondary governing bodies of the regnum. Was it a return to the duality of the Lares? When Titus Tatius of Cures was killed in obscure circumstances in Lavinium, the delicate balance became undone. Romulus, accused of having seized absolute power, was likewise killed, and a successor was named in compensation, another Sabine from Cures: Numa Pompilius. In this succession, too, we glimpse a sort of rebalancing of power.

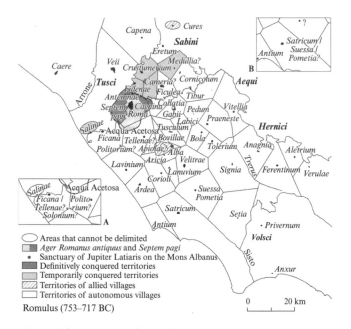

Fig. 60. The conquests of Romulus.

Romulus alone conquered first Crustumerium and Medullia, and then—after Titus Tatius was gone—Fidenae, the Septem Pagi, and the Salinae. Together Romulus and Titus Tatius conquered Cameria (fig. 60). Of these conquests, the only definitive ones were those achieved within the traditional *ager* and that of the Septem Pagi, as a result of which Veii was forced to scale back its frontier. The other centers and places would have to reconquered. We note that the first wars were fought on two fronts, the first front being that separating the originally Latin cities situated between the Aniene River and the Sabines—alarming the Sabines and provoking their reaction—and the second front involving Veii. On the other hand, there was no front by the sea, which would later become the principal front under Ancus Marcius, the fourth king of Rome and founder of Ostia, under whose reign the territory of Rome would finally equal and surpass that of Veii (fig. 61). Rome's third king, Tullus Hostilius, had put an end to the fortress of Alba Longa, and thenceforth the sacred metropolis of the Latins would be Lavinium, by the sea.

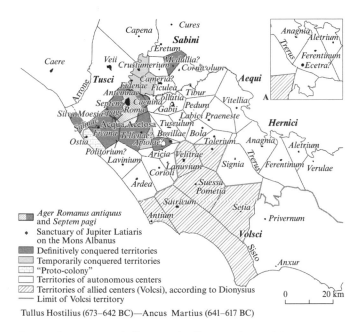

Tullus Hostilius (673–642 BC)—Ancus Martius (641–617 BC)

Fig. 61. Conquests and alliances of Tullus Hostilius and Ancus Marcius.

CONCLUSION

After twenty years of excavations between the Palatine and the Forum and studies on the birth of Rome, we were able to ascertain that the structural data that could be gleaned from the legend of Remus and Romulus, from the *constitutio Romuli*, and from the early Roman calendar converge and harmonize with what can be gleaned from older excavations upon reexamination, and especially from the new excavations that we ourselves have conducted. This realization led us to conclude that the settlement of the Quirites—the enlargement of the Septimontium to the *colles*—had endowed itself, as of the second quarter of the eighth century BC, with an *urbs*, a forum, a citadel (arx), and an *ager*, which together formed a regnum—that is, a *res publica*, what today we would call a state—governed by a *rex* and by other, secondary powers, in accordance with a sacred, juridical, and political dispensation of a constitutional character. The new excavations, moreover, make it possible to assert that the city-state was realized in a brief span of time, between 777/750 BC and 700/675 BC, and perfected between 675 and 625 BC, after which came the new age of the Tarquini and the constitutional reform of Servius Tullius, which is dated from circa 575–550 BC and survived intact until the end of the sixth century BC, when the Republic was established.

Defending contrary theses will now be the task of the usual sectors of contemporary historiography, which, on the basis of overly limited and inadequately conducted and published excavations still maintains, though with diminishing persuasiveness, that the first city-state was created much later, between circa 625 and 550 BC.

───── ❦ ─────

And so the time has come to return from the twenty-seven and a half centuries in which we had buried ourselves until now and to ask ourselves if any historical link or identity still ties us to the first Romans, or if Romulus is like a primitive king from any other part of the world for us.

I believe that our connection with the pagan world of our origins—the time of Homer and Romulus—is still alive and lies in the discovery first made by the ancients in Greece, Etruria, and Rome of a particular way of organizing life, a sacral-juridical-political-governmental model according to which the different governing bodies of the community (the king, the aristocracy, and the people) manage to live together by mitigating centralized power within a unique form of organization, which we can call, as the ancients did, a "mixed constitution."

This involves the very difficult art of living in concord, beyond all differences, and existing separately without considering one another an enemy. Elsewhere I have called this *savoir vivre* the "Western syndrome."[1] We see its most distant root in the *civitas*/regnum of early-archaic Rome, understood as a *res publica*, after having been a monarchy at its beginnings. The so-called Western syndrome is a simplification whereby we can compare—crudely but efficiently—the preeminent character of Western history to the contrary "Eastern syndrome," which is based intrinsically on cities and kingdoms and perpetually despotic in character. The West, too, has known tyrannies, dominations, absolutisms, and dictatorships, which denatured the Western model with Eastern-style mechanisms. On the whole, however, over the centuries these Eastern solutions have not prevailed, allowing, at the end of a long and conflict-filled journey, democracies to be reborn and develop. In the twentieth century, democracies have been grafted onto a number of Asian societies, such as India and Japan, managing miraculously to take root; but these are exceptions, while the absence of a multilayered Western syndrome continues to favor despotism. Perhaps Eastern countries need first to find their own way to the Western syndrome before they can walk among the democracies?

---

[1] A. Carandini, *Sindrome occidentale* (Genoa: Il Melangolo, 2007).

Some contemporary historians criticize the ancient democ-racies for their incompleteness, as if they were nothing more than oligarchies in disguise, confusing political formations— inevitably imperfect—with ideal models unattainable except through despotism. In so doing, these historians end up justi-fying the horrors of modern fascist and communist dictator-ships, pointing out the temporary consensus on which they were based. Western democracies are certainly full of defects, but they have the advantage of being perfectible, and in many respects they have indeed perfected themselves. I suspect it is unlikely that anything better will emerge from the lands of the rising sun.

The ancient city-state was based on a site of civic worship in an elevated place, with a political center situated around a public square on lower ground (*agorà, forum*). For as long as constitutional monarchic forms, and the limited-term magis-tratures derived from them, lasted, royal residences in Greece and Italy, from the early-archaic to the archaic age, remained dignified but modest constructions—not more than 620 square meters in area (fig. 62). In contrast, Eastern cities were and are still centered around palaces and "forbidden" quar-ters greater than one hectare in area, and often far greater, such as in Beijing (fig. 64), in sharp contrast to 10 Downing Street (fig. 63).

Following the Dark Ages, starting around the ninth and tenth centuries AD, city-states reemerged, especially in Italy,

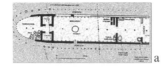

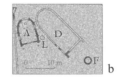

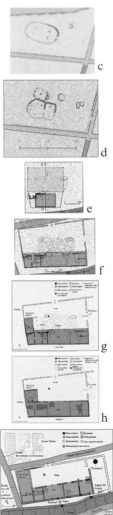

Fig. 62. Eastern, Greek, and Roman royal residences:
(a) Lefkandi, Euboea, king's hut; (b) Eretria, Euboea,
hut of the basileus, Temple of Apollo, and altar; (c) hut
on the Cermalus (cf. fig. 21); (d) hut and sacrarium on
the Cermalus (cf. fig. 20); (e) tabernaculum/*casa* in the
Sanctuary of Vesta (cf. fig. 32); (f–i) Domus Regia in
the Sanctuary of Vesta (cf. figs. 35, 37–39). *Lower left*
(not to scale): Crete, Knossos Palace.

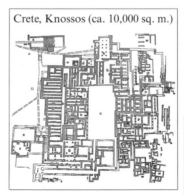

Crete, Knossos (ca. 10,000 sq. m.)

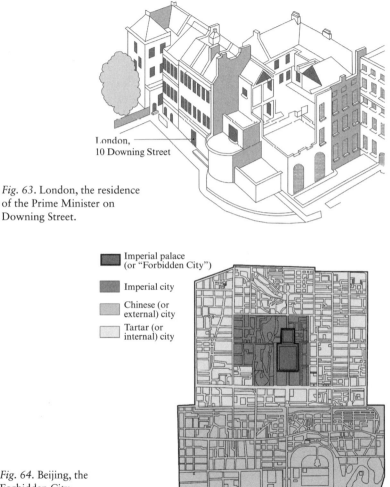

London,
10 Downing Street

Fig. 63. London, the residence
of the Prime Minister on
Downing Street.

Imperial palace
(or "Forbidden City")

Imperial city

Chinese (or
external) city

Tartar (or
internal) city

Fig. 64. Beijing, the
Forbidden City.

and remained such until the modern era, whereas in the rest of Europe, great kingdoms were formed. The Magna Cartas in Northern Italy and England, and the States-General in France, date from between 1107 and 1303. Our pre-Christian identity thus concerns not only the *ius* of the Romans, as is generally believed, but also the broader political-constitutional-governmental model that I have defined as the "Western syndrome."

Literary Sources[1]
Edited by Paolo Carafa

———⊛———

THE PALATINE

ENNIUS, *ANNALS*

And so with great speed in their readiness, and wishing
to rule, together they turn their minds to auspices and augury.
Upon the mount sits Remus for the auspice, and alone
he awaits the auspicious bird; good Romulus seeks instead   75
his sign atop the Aventine, awaiting the brood of high-flyers.
They were vying to see if the town would be called Rome or
    Remora.
All their men wondered who would become king.
They wait, as when the consul is about to give the sign,
and all watch the thresholds of the stores in eagerness,   80
to see when the chariots will come out through the painted
    doors;
thus the people awaited and looked anxious to see
to which brother events would grant victory over the great
    realm.
Meanwhile the bright sun had stirred in the depths of night
and again the clear light cast out by the rays had shone;   85
then from above, of the utmost beauty, and swift,

a bird flies from the left, and at once the golden sun rises.
But now from the sky approach thrice four holy bodies of
   birds,
and they repair to auspicious, favorable places.
Thus does Romulus know that the auspice has granted   90
to him alone the stable throne of the realm and the soil.
(I fr. xlvii. Skutsch, ll. 72–91. Translation by Stephen Sartarelli.)

Dionysius of Halicarnassus, *The Roman Antiquities*

85, 1. I am now going to relate the events that happened at the
very time of its founding; for this part of my account still remains.
When Numitor, upon the death of Amulius, had resumed his rule
and had spent a little time in restoring the city from its late disorder to its former orderly state, he presently thought of providing
an independent rule for the youths by founding another city. 2. At
the same time, the inhabitants being much increased in number, he
thought it good policy to get rid of some part of them, particularly
of those who had once been his enemies, lest he might have cause
to suspect any of his subjects. And having communicated this plan
to the youths and gained their approval, he gave them, as a district to rule, the region where they had been brought up in their
infancy, and, for subjects, not only that part of the people which
he suspected of a design to begin rebellion anew, but also any who
were willing to migrate voluntarily. 3. Among these, as is likely to
happen when a city sends out a colony, there were great numbers
of the common people, but there were also a sufficient number of

the prominent men of the best class, and of the Trojan element all those who were esteemed the noblest in birth, some of whose posterity remained even to my day, consisting of about fifty families. The youths were supplied with money, arms and corn, with slaves and beasts of burden and everything else that was of use in the building of a city. 4. After they had led their people out of Alba and intermingled with them the local population that still remained in Pallantium and Saturnia, they divided the whole multitude into two parts. This they did in the hope of arousing a spirit of emulation, so that through their rivalry with each other their tasks might be the sooner finished; however, it produced the greatest of evils, discord. 5. For each group, exalting its own leader, extolled him as the proper person to command them all; and the youths themselves, being now no longer one in mind or feeling it necessary to entertain brotherly sentiments toward each, since each expected to command the other, scorned equality and craved superiority. For some time their ambitions were concealed, but later they burst forth on the occasion which I shall now describe. 6. They did not both favour the same site for the building of the city; for Romulus proposed to settle the Palatine hill, among other reasons, because of the good fortune of the place where they had been preserved and brought up, whereas Remus favoured the place that is now named after him, Remoria. And indeed this place is very suitable for a city, being a hill not far from the Tiber and about thirty stades from Rome. From this rivalry their unsociable love of rule immediately began to disclose itself; for on the one who now yielded the victor would inevitably impose his will on all occasions alike.

86, 1. Meanwhile, some time having elapsed and their discord in no degree abating, the two agreed to refer the matter to their grandfather and for that purpose went to Alba. He advised them to leave it to the decision of the gods which of them should give his name to the colony and be its leader. And having appointed for them a day, he ordered them to place themselves early in the morning at a distance from one another, in such stations as each of them should think proper, and after first offering to the gods the customary sacrifices, to watch for auspicious birds; and he ordered that he to whom the more favourable birds first appeared should rule the colony. 2. The youths, approving of this, went away and according to their agreement appeared on the day appointed for the test. Romulus chose for his station the Palatine hill, where he proposed settling the colony, and Remus the Aventine hill adjoining it, or, according to others, Remoria; and a guard attended them both, to prevent their reporting things otherwise than as they appeared. 3. When they had taken their respective stations, Romulus, after a short pause, from eagerness and jealousy of his brother, — though possibly Heaven was thus directing him, — even before he saw any omen at all, sent messengers to his brother desiring him to come immediately, as if he had been the first to see some auspicious birds. But while the persons he sent were proceeding with no great haste, feeling ashamed of the fraud, six vultures appeared to Remus, flying from the right; and he, seeing the birds, rejoiced greatly. And not long afterwards the men sent by Romulus took him thence and brought him to the Palatine hill. 4. When they were together, Remus asked Romulus what birds he had been the first to see, and Romulus knew not what to answer. But thereupon twelve auspicious vultures were seen flying; and upon seeing these he took courage, and pointing them out to Remus, said: "Why do you demand to know what happened a long time ago? For surely you see these birds yourself." But Remus was indignant and complained bitterly because he had been deceived by him; and he refused to yield to him his right to the colony.

87, 1. Thereupon greater strife arose between them than before, as each, while secretly striving for the advantage, was ostensibly willing to accept equality, for the following reason. Their grandfather, as I have stated, had ordered that he to whom the more favourable birds first appeared should rule the colony; but, as the same kind of birds had been seen by both, one had the advantage of seeing them first and the other that of seeing the greater number. The rest of the people also espoused their quarrel, and arming themselves without orders from their leaders, began war; and a sharp battle ensued in which many were slain on both sides. 2. In the course of this battle, as some say, Faustulus, who had brought up the youths, wishing to put an end to the strife of the brothers and being unable to do so, threw himself unarmed into the midst of the combatants, seeking the speediest death, which fell out accordingly. Some say also that the stone lion which stood in the principal part of the Forum near the rostra was placed over the body of Faustulus, who was buried by those who found him in the place where he fell. 3. Remus having been slain in this action, Romulus, who had gained a most melancholy victory through the death of his brother and the mutual slaughter of citizens, buried Remus at Remoria, since when alive he had clung to it as the site for the new city. As for himself, in his grief and repentance for what had happened, he became dejected and lost all desire for life. But when Laurentia, who had received the babes when newly born and brought them up and loved them no less than a mother, entreated and comforted him, he listened to her and rose up, and gathering together the Latins who had not been slain in the battle (they were now little more than three thousand out of a very great multitude at first, when he led out the colony), he built a city on the Palatine hill.

4.The account I have given seems to me the most probable of the stories about the death of Remus.

(I 85–87, 4. Translation by Ernest Cary, from Dionysius of Halicarnassus, *The Roman Antiquities*, Loeb Classical Library [Cambridge, MA: Harvard University Press, 1937–1950], http://penelope.uchicago.edu/ Thayer/E/Roman/Texts/Dionysius_of_Halicarnassus/1D*.html.)

Livy, *The History of Rome*

6, 3. After the government of Alba was thus transferred to Numitor, Romulus and Remus were seized with the desire of building a city in the locality where they had been exposed. There was the superfluous population of the Alban and Latin towns, to these were added the shepherds: it was natural to hope that with all these Alba would be small and Lavinium small in comparison with the city which was to be founded. 4. These pleasant anticipations were disturbed by the ancestral curse—ambition—which led to a deplorable quarrel over what was at first a trivial matter. As they were twins and no claim to precedence could be based on seniority, they decided to consult the tutelary deities of the place by means of augury as to who was to give his name to the new city, and who was to rule it after it had been founded. Romulus accordingly selected the Palatine as his station for observation, Remus the Aventine.

7, 1. Remus is said to have been the first to receive an omen: six vultures appeared to him. The augury had just been announced to Romulus when double the number appeared to him. Each was saluted as king by his own party. 2. The one side based their claim on the priority of the appearance, the other on the number of the birds. Then followed an angry altercation; heated passions led to bloodshed; in the tumult Remus was killed. . . .

(I, 1, 6–7. Translation by Rev. Canon Roberts, from Titus Livius, *The History of Rome*, edited by Ernest Rhys, Everyman's Library [London: J. M. Dent and Sons, New York: E. P. Dutton and Co., 1912], http://etext .lib.virginia.edu/toc/modeng/public/Liv1His.html.)

Ovid, *Fasti*

Amulius had already been punished, and all	
The shepherd folk were subject to the twins,	810
Who agreed to gather the men together to build walls:	
The question was as to which of them should do it.	
Romulus said: "There's no need to fight about it:	
Great faith is placed in birds, let's judge by birds."	
That seemed fine. One tried the rocks of the wooded	
Palatine,	815
The other climbed at dawn to the Aventine's summit.	
Remus saw six birds, Romulus twelve in a row.	

(IV, 809–817. Translation by A. S. Kline, © 2004,

http://www.poetryintranslation.com/PITBR/Latin/Fastihome.htm.)

Plutarch, *Romulus*

1. Amulius now being dead and matters quietly disposed, the two brothers would neither dwell in Alba without governing there, nor take the government into their own hands during the life of their grandfather. Having therefore delivered the dominion up into his hands, and paid their mother befitting honour, they resolved to live by themselves, and build a city in the same place where they were in their infancy brought up. This seems the most honourable reason for their departure; 2. though perhaps it was necessary, having such a body of slaves and fugitives collected about them, either to come to nothing by dispersing them, or if not so, then to live with them elsewhere. For that the inhabitants of Alba did not think fugitives worthy of being received and incorporated as citizens among them plainly appears from the matter of the women, an attempt made not wantonly but of necessity, because they could not get wives by goodwill. For they certainly paid unusual respect and honour to those whom they thus forcibly seized.

3. Not long after the first foundation of the city, they opened a sanctuary of refuge for all fugitives, which they called the temple of the god Asylaeus, where they received and protected all, delivering none back, neither the servant to his master, the debtor to his creditor, nor the murderer into the hands of the magistrate, saying it was a privileged place, and they could so maintain it by an order of the holy oracle; insomuch that the city grew presently very populous,

for they say, it consisted at first of no more than a thousand houses. But of that hereafter.

4. Their minds being full bent upon building, there arose presently a difference about the place. Romulus chose what was called Roma Quadrata, or the Square Rome, and would have the city there. Remus laid out a piece of ground on the Aventine Mount, well fortified by nature, which was from him called Remonium, but now Rignarium. 5. Concluding at last to decide the contest by a divination from a flight of birds, and placing themselves apart at some distance. Remus, they say, saw six vultures, and Romulus double that number; others say, Remus did truly see his number, and that Romulus feigned his, but when Remus came to him, that then he did indeed see twelve. Hence it is that the Romans, in their divinations from birds, chiefly regard the vulture. . . .

(IX, 1–5. Translation by John Dryden et al., from Plutarch, *Parallel Lives*, http://classics.mit.edu/Plutarch/romulus.html.)

Servius, *Commentary on Virgil's* Aeneid

Having taken the auguries, Romulus cast a spear from the Aventine hill towards the Palatine; and, penetrating the earth, it grew branches and became a tree.

(III, 46 [S. S.])

THE BLESSING OF THE PALATINE AND FOUNDATION OF THE ROMA QUADRATA

Dionysius of Halicarnassus, *The Roman Antiquities*

88, 1. When no obstacle now remained to the building of the city, Romulus appointed a day on which he planned to begin the work, after first propitiating the gods. And having prepared everything that would be required for the sacrifices and for the entertainment of the people, when the appointed time came, he himself first offered sacrifice to the gods and ordered all the rest to do the same according to their abilities. He then in the first place took the omens, which were favourable. After that, having commanded fires to be lighted before the tents, he caused the people to come out and leap over the flames in order to expiate their guilt. 2. When he thought everything had been done which he conceived to be acceptable to the gods, he called all the people to the appointed place and described a quadrangular figure about the hill, tracing with a plough drawn by a bull and a cow yoked together a continuous furrow designed to receive the foundation of the wall; and from that time this custom has continued among the Romans of ploughing a furrow round the site where they plan to build a city. After he had done this and sacrificed the bull and the cow and also performed the initial rites over many other victims, he set the people to work. 3. This day the Romans celebrate every year even down to my time as one of their greatest festivals and call it the Parilia. On this day, which comes in the beginning of spring, the husbandmen and herdsmen offer up a sacrifice of thanksgiving for the increase of their cattle. But whether they had celebrated this day in even earlier times as a day of rejoicing and for that reason looked upon it as the most suitable for the founding of the city, or whether, because it marked the beginning of the building of the city, they consecrated it and thought they should honour on it the gods who are propitious to shepherds, I cannot say for certain.

(I, 88, 1–3 [E. C.])

Ovid, *Fasti*

A day was chosen for him to mark out the walls with a
    plough.
The festival of Pales was near: the work was started then.   820
They trenched to the solid rock, threw fruits of the harvest
Into its depths, with soil from the ground nearby.
The ditch was filled with earth, and topped by an altar,
And a fire was duly kindled on the new-made hearth.
Then, bearing down on the plough handle, he marked the
    walls: 825
The yoke was borne by a white cow and a snowy ox.
So spoke the king: "Be with me, as I found my City,
Jupiter, Father Mavors, and Mother Vesta:
And all you gods, whom piety summons, take note.
Let my work be done beneath your auspices.   830
May it last long, and rule a conquered world,
All subject, from the rising to the setting day."
Jupiter added his omen to Romulus' prayer, with thunder
On the left, and his lightning flashed leftward in the sky.
Delighted by this, the citizens laid foundations,   835

And the new walls were quickly raised.
(IV, ll. 819–836 [A.S.K.])

Tacitus, *Annals*

24. There are various popular accounts of the ambitious and vain-glorious efforts of our kings in this matter [i.e., concerning the right to enlarge the city]. Still, I think, it is interesting to know accurately the original plan of the precinct (*pomerium*), as it was fixed by Romulus. From the ox market, where we see the brazen statue of a bull, because that animal is yoked to the plough, a furrow was drawn to mark out the town, so as to embrace the great altar of Hercules; then, at regular intervals, stones were placed along the foot of the Palatine hill to the altar of Consus, soon afterwards, to the old Courts, and then to the chapel of Larunda. The Roman forum and the Capitol were not, it was supposed, added to the city by Romulus, but by Titus Tatius. In time, the precinct (*pomerium*) was enlarged with the growth of Rome's fortunes. . . .

(XII, 24. Translation by Alfred John Church and William Jackson Brod-ribb, from *The Complete Works of Tacitus*, edited by Moses Hadas [New York: Modern Library, 1942].)

Plutarch, *Romulus*

11, 1. Romulus, having buried his brother Remus, together with his two foster-fathers, on the mount Remonia, set to building his city; and sent for men out of Tuscany, who directed him by sacred usages and written rules in all the ceremonies to be observed, as in a religious rite. 2. First, they dug a round trench about that which is now the Comitium, or Court of Assembly, and into it solemnly threw the first-fruits of all things either good by custom or necessary by nature; lastly, every man taking a small piece of earth of the country from whence he came, they all threw in promiscuously together. This trench they call, as they do the heavens, Mundus; making which their centre, they described the city in a circle round it. 3. Then the founder fitted to a plough a brazen ploughshare, and, yoking together a bull and a cow, drove himself a deep line or furrow round the bounds; while the business of those that followed after was to see that whatever earth was thrown up should be turned all inwards towards the city; and not to let any clod lie outside. 4. With this line they described the wall, and called it, by a contraction, Pomoerium, that is, postmurum, after or beside the wall; and where they designed to make a gate, there they took out the share, carried the plough over, and left a space; 5. for which reason they consider the whole wall as holy, except where the gates are; for had they adjudged them also sacred, they could not, without offence to religion, have given free ingress and egress for the necessaries of human life, some of which are in themselves unclean.

12, 1. As for the day they began to build the city, it is universally agreed to have been the twenty-first of April, and that day the Romans annually keep holy, calling it their country's birthday. At first, they say, they sacrificed no living creature on this day, thinking it fit to preserve the feast of their country's birthday pure and without stain of blood. 2. Yet before ever the city was built, there was a feast of herdsmen and shepherds kept on this day, which went by the name of Palilia. The Roman and Greek months have now little or no agreement; they say, however, the day on which Romulus began to build was quite certainly the thirtieth of the month, at which time there was an eclipse of the sun which they conceived to be that seen by Antimachus, the Teian poet, in the third year of the sixth Olympiad.

(XI, 1–5; XII, 1–2 [Dryden et al.])

Gellius, *Attic Nights*

Now, the most ancient pomerium, which was established by Romulus, was bounded by the foot of the Palatine hill.

(XIII, 14, 2. Translation by J. C. Rolfe, from Gellius, *Attic Nights*, vol. 2, Loeb Classical Library [Cambridge, MA: Harvard University Press, 1927], http://penelope.uchicago.edu/Thayer/E/Roman/Texts/Gellius/home.html.)

John the Lydian, *The Months*

Eleven days before the Calends of May, Romulus founded Rome, after gathering together all the inhabitants of the nearby areas and ordering them to bring with them a clod of their own soil, to augur that Rome should dominate the whole region. As for himself, after imposing himself as leader of the entire sacred function, and taking a sacred horn—by ancestral tradition the Romans call it a *lituus*, from *lité*, meaning "prayer"—let the name of the city ring out. The city had three names—one initiatory, one sacred, and one political—the initiatory name is Love [Amor], that is, Eros, so that all might be pervaded by a divine love of the city, the reason why the poet, in his bucolic songs, enigmatically calls it Amaryllis; the sacred name is Flora, that is, "blossoming," from which derives the feast of the Floralia in her honor; and the political name is Rome. The political name was known to all and was uttered without fear, while only the supreme pontiffs were allowed to pronounce her initiatory name, during sacred rites; and it is said that once, a magistrate was punished for having dared to make the initiatory name known to the public.

After proclaiming the city, having yoked an adult bull with a heifer, Romulus traced a circle round the walls, having placed the male bovine on the side of the fields and the female on the side of the city, so that the males would terrorize those who were outside the city and the females would give birth to those within the walls. And, taking up a clod of earth from outside the city, he cast this toward the inside, along with the clods brought by the others, thus ensuring that the city would grow at the expense of those outside, without pause, and in a short time. As many strangers arrived in the city, the men chosen by Romulus conceded half of their possessions to them, persuading them to live in Rome; and Romulus first called them "patricians," because they descended from noble fathers and had given their wealth to strangers for the good of the fatherland.

(IV, 73 [S. S.])

Zonaras

Having buried his brother, Romulus set about founding the city; after yoking an ox and a heifer and affixing a bronze blade to the plough, he carved a deep circular furrow, while the others, following behind, threw back into the furrow all the clods of earth raised by the plough. And the furrow was traced at the place where the walls were to be raised, as has been said, while where they thought to build gates, the furrow was interrupted, by raising the plough up. Indeed, the entire wall is held sacred; if all the walls had been held sacred, it would not have been allowed for necessary things to pass through, for they are nevertheless impure. The founding of the city was completed eleven days before the calends of May, which is to say, on the twentieth day of April. And the Romans celebrate this day, calling it the birthday of their country. Tradition states that Romulus was eighteen years old when he founded Rome; he situated her near the house of Faustulus, and the place was called the Palatine.

(VII, 3 [S. S.])

THE FOUNDING OF THE FORUM, THE CAPITOL, AND THE CITADEL

The Forum

Ovid, *Fasti*

The ground was soft at dawn, with a frost of dew:
When the crowd gathered at the king's threshold.
He emerged, and sat in the midst on a maple wood throne.
Countless warriors stood around him in silence.   360
Phoebus had scarcely risen above the horizon:
Their anxious minds trembled with hope and fear.
The king stood, his head covered with a white cloth
Raising his hands, that the god now knew so well.
He spoke as follows: "The time is here for the promised

gift,   365

Jupiter, make true the words of your pledge."

As he spoke, the sun's full disc appeared,

And a loud crash came from the depths of the sky.

Three times the god thundered, and hurled his lightning,

From cloudless air, believe what I say, wonderful but

    true.   370

The sky began to split open at the zenith:

The crowd and its leader lifted their eyes.

Behold, a shield fell, trembling in the light breeze.

The sound of the crowd's shouting reached the stars.

The king first sacrificed a heifer that had never known   375

The yoke, then raised the gift from the ground,

And called it *ancile*, because it was cut away (*recisum*)

All round, and there wasn't a single angle to note.

(III, ll. 357–378 [A.S.K.])

Dionysius of Halicarnassus, *The Roman Antiquities*

65, 1. At any rate, as regards the building of the temple of Vesta, some ascribe it to Romulus, looking upon it as an inconceivable thing that, when a city was being founded by a man skilled in divination, a public hearth should not have been erected first of all, particularly since the founder had been brought up at Alba, where the temple of this goddess had been established from ancient times, and since his mother had been her priestess.

(II 65, 1 [E. C.])

Dionysius of Halicarnassus, *The Roman Antiquities*

50, 1. Romulus and Tatius immediately enlarged the city by adding
to it two other hills, the Quirinal, as it is called, and the Caelian;
and separating their habitations, each of them had his particular
place of residence. Romulus occupied the Palatine and Caelian hills,
the latter being next to the Palatine, and Tatius the Capitoline hill,
which he had seized in the beginning, and the Quirinal. 2. And cut-
ting down the wood that grew on the plain at the foot of the Capitoline and filling up the greatest part of the lake, which, since it lay
in a hollow, was kept well supplied by the waters that came down
from the hills, they converted the plain into a forum, which the
Romans continue to use even now; there they held their assemblies,
transacting their business in the temple of Vulcan, which stands a
little above the Forum.

(II, 50, 1–2 [E. C.])

Plutarch, *Romulus*

9. Upon this, conditions were agreed upon, that what women
pleased might stay where they were, exempt, as aforesaid, from all
drudgery and labour but spinning; that the Romans and Sabines
should inhabit the city together; that the city should be called Rome
from Romulus; but the Romans, Quirites, from the country of Tatius; and that they both should govern and command in common.
10. The place of the ratification is still called Comitium, from come
to meet.

(XIX, 9–10 [Dryden et al.])

Cassius Dio

... [T]hey [i.e., the Romans and Sabines] who listened to them and saw them, burst into tears, ceased their quarrel, whereupon [they] went together to negotiate in the place which for this reason was called *comitium*.

(5, 5 Boissevain [S. S.])

THE ORDERING OF THE REGNUM, OR THE *CONSTITUTIO ROMULI*

THE ORDERING OF TIME

Gellius, *Attic Nights*

When I had brought this matter to the attention of several scholars, some of them argued that in Homer's time, as in that of Romulus, the year consisted, not of twelve months, but of ten.

(III, 16, 16 [J.C.R.])

John the Lydian, *The Months*

From Kronos until the foundation of Rome, the year was continually observed according to the phases of the moon, and it was measured by Romulus ... in ten months, some with thirty-one days, some with thirty days. Indeed they did not yet measure time by the movements of the sun.

(I, 16 [S. S.])

Censorinus

It is true that Licinius Macro and later Fenestella wrote that the solar year, from the start, was twelve months long; but we must lend more credence to Junius Graccanus, Fulvius, Varro, Suetonius, and others, who think that it was ten months long, as it was for the Albani, from whom the Romans descended.

(XX, 2 [S. S.])

Chronographus anni CCCLIIII

Romulus, son of Mars and Sylvia, reigned for 38 years. . . . He established a year of ten months, from March to December.

(IX, 1. MGH-AA, Mommsen, ed., p. 144. [S. S.])

THE ORDERING OF SPACE AND MEN

Cicero, *The Commonwealth*

After the death of Tatius, the entire government was again vested in the hands of Romulus. This monarch had, however, even during the lifetime of Tatius, formed a royal council or senate of the chief noblemen, who were entitled by the affection of the people Patres, or Patricians. He also formed Comitia, or a house of Commons, by dividing the people into three tribes, nominated after the name of Tatius, his own name, and that of Lucumon his friend, who had fallen in the Sabine war. He likewise made another division of the people into thirty Curiæ, designated by the names of those Sabine virgins, who after being carried off at the festivals, generously offered themselves as the mediators of peace and coalition.

But though these orders were established in the life of Tatius, yet after his death, Romulus reigned in double power by the council and authority of the senate.

(II, vii, 14. Translation by Francis Barham, from *The Political Works of Marcus Tullius Cicero: Comprising his Treatise on the Commonwealth; and his Treatise on the Laws* [London: Edmund Spettigue, 1841–42], vol. 1, http://oll.libertyfund.org/?option=com_staticxt&staticfile=show.php%3 Ftitle=546&chapter=83299&layout=html&Itemid=27.)

Dionysius of Halicarnassus, *The Roman Antiquities*

7, 1. Romulus, who was thus chosen king by both men and gods, is allowed to have been a man of great military ability and personal bravery and of the greatest sagacity in instituting the best kind of government. I shall relate such of his political and military achievements as may be thought worthy of mention in a history; 2. and first I shall speak of the form of government that he instituted, which I regard as the most self-sufficient of all political systems both for peace and for war. This was the plan of it: He divided all the people into three groups, and set over each as leader its most distinguished man. Then he subdivided each of these three groups into ten others, and appointed as many of the bravest men to be the leaders of these also. The larger divisions he called tribes and the smaller curiae, as they are still termed even in our day. 3. These names may be translated into Greek as follows: a tribe by phylê and trittys, and a curia by phratra and lochos; the commanders of the tribes, whom the Romans call tribunes, by phylarchoi and trittyarchoi; and the commanders of the curiae, whom they call curiones, by phratriarchoi and lochagoi. 4. These curiae were again divided by him into ten parts, each commanded by its own leader, who was called decurio in the native language. The people being thus divided and assigned to tribes and curiae, he divided the land into thirty equal portions and assigned one of them to each curia, having first set apart as much of it as was sufficient for the support of the temples and shrines and also reserved some part of the land for the use of the public. This was one division made by Romulus, both of the men and of the land, which involved the greatest equality for all alike.

(II, 7, 1–4 [E. C.])

Dionysius of Halicarnassus, *The Roman Antiquities*

12, 1. As soon as Romulus had regulated these matters he determined to appoint senators to assist him in administering the public business, and to this end he chose a hundred men from among the patricians, selecting them in the following manner. He himself appointed one, the best out of their whole number, to whom he thought fit to entrust the government of the city whenever he himself should lead the army beyond the borders. 2. He next ordered each of the tribes to choose three men who were then at the age of greatest prudence and were distinguished by their birth. After these nine were chosen he ordered each curia likewise to name three patricians who were the most worthy. Then adding to the first nine, who had been named by the tribes, the ninety who were chosen by the curiae, and appointing as their head the man he himself had first selected, he completed the number of a hundred senators. 3. The name of this council may be expressed in Greek by gerousia or "council of elders," and it is called by the Romans to this day; but whether it received its name from the advanced age of the men who were appointed to it or from their merit, I cannot say for certain. For the ancients used to call the older men and those of greatest merit gerontes or "elders." The members of the senate were called Conscript Fathers, and they retained that name down to my time. This council, also, was a Greek institution. 4. At any rate, the Greek kings, both those who inherited the realms of their ancestors and those who were elected by the people themselves to be their rulers, had a council composed of the best men, as both Homer and the most ancient of the poets testify; and the authority of the ancient kings was not arbitrary and absolute as it is in our days.

(II, 12, 1–4 [E. C.])

Dionysius of Halicarnassus, *The Roman Antiquities*

14, 1. Having made these regulations, he distinguished the honours and powers which he wished each class to have. For the king he had reserved these prerogatives: in the first place, the supremacy in religious ceremonies and sacrifices and the conduct of everything relating to the worship of the gods; secondly, the guardianship of the laws and customs of the country and the general oversight of justice in all cases, whether founded on the law of nature or the civil law; he was also the judge in person [for] the greatest crimes, leaving the lesser to the senators, but seeing to it that no error was made in their decisions; he was to summon the senate and call together the popular assembly, to deliver his opinion first and carry out the decision of the majority. These prerogatives he granted to the king and, in addition, the absolute command in war.

(II, 14, 1 [E. C.])

Dionysius of Halicarnassus, *The Roman Antiquities*

14, 3. To the populace he granted these three privileges: to choose magistrates, to ratify laws, and to decide concerning war whenever the king left the decision to them; yet even in these matters their authority was not unrestricted, since the concurrence of the senate was necessary to give effect to their decisions. The people did not give their votes all at the same time, but were summoned to meet by curiae, and whatever was resolved upon by the majority of the curiae was reported to the senate. But in our day this practice is reversed, since the senate does not deliberate upon the resolutions passed by the people, but the people have full power over the decrees of the senate; and which of the two customs is better I leave it open to others to determine.

(II, 14, 3 [E. C.])

Livy, *The History of Rome*

1. After the claims of religion had been duly acknowledged, Romulus called his people to a council. As nothing could unite them into one political body but the observance of common laws and customs, he gave them a body of laws, 2.which he thought would only

be respected by a rude and uncivilised race of men if he inspired them with awe by assuming the outward symbols of power. He surrounded himself with greater state, and in particular he called into his service twelve lictors. 3. Some think that he fixed upon this number from the number of the birds who foretold his sovereignty; but I am inclined to agree with those who think that as this class of public officers was borrowed from the same people from whom the "sella curulis" and the "toga praetexta" were adopted—their neighbours, the Etruscans—so the number itself also was taken from them. Its use amongst the Etruscans is traced to the custom of the twelve sovereign cities of Etruria, when jointly electing a king, furnishing him each with one lictor.

(I, 8, 1–3 [R.C.R.])

Sextus Pomponius, *Digesta*

After the city increased somewhat in size, it is said that Romulus divided the people into thirteen parts, which he called curiae, because at the time he administered the care (*cura*) of the state according to the counsel of those parts. Thus he himself proposed certain curiate laws, which remain recorded in the book of Sextius Papirius, a notable man who lived at the time of Superbus, son of Demaratus of Corinth. This book, as we have said, is called the *Civil Law of Papirius*, not because Papirius added anything of his own thereto, but because he organized in a single body laws that had been issued in no order.

(I, 2, 2 [S. S.])

ENEMIES

Dionysius of Halicarnassus, *The Roman Antiquities*

87, 4. The account I have given seems to me the most probable of the stories about the death of Remus. However, if any has been handed down that differs from this, let that also be related. Some, indeed, say that Remus yielded the leadership to Romulus, though not without resentment and anger at the fraud, but that after the wall was built, wishing to demonstrate the weakness of the fortification, he cried, "Well, as for this wall, one of your enemies could as easily cross it as I do," and immediately leaped over it. Thereupon Celer, one of the men standing on the wall, who was overseer of the work, said, "Well, as for this enemy, one of us could easily punish him," and striking him on the head with a mattock, he killed him then and there. Such is said to have been the outcome of the quarrel between the brothers.

(I, 87, 4 [E. C.])

Livy, *The History of Rome*

2. The more common report is that Remus contemptuously jumped over the newly raised walls and was forthwith killed by the enraged Romulus, who exclaimed, "So shall it be henceforth with every one who leaps over my walls." 3. Romulus thus became sole ruler, and the city was called after him, its founder. His first work was to fortify the Palatine hill where he had been brought up.

(I, 7, 2–3 [R.C.R.])

Ovid, *Fasti*

The work was overseen by Celer, whom Romulus named,
Saying: "Celer, make it your care to see no one crosses
Walls or trench that we've ploughed: kill whoever dares."   840
Remus, unknowingly, began to mock the low walls,
saying: "Will the people be safe behind these?"
He leapt them, there and then. Celer struck the rash man
With his shovel: Remus sank, bloodied, to the stony ground.
When the king heard, he smothered his rising tears,   845
And kept the grief locked in his heart.
He wouldn't weep in public, but set an example of fortitude,
Saying: "So dies the enemy who shall cross my walls."
(IV, 837–848 [A.S.K.])

Plutarch, *Romulus*

1. When Remus knew the cheat [i.e., by Romulus], he was much displeased; and as Romulus was casting up a ditch, where he designed the foundation of the city-wall, he turned some pieces of the work to ridicule, and obstructed others; 2. at last, as he was in contempt leaping over it, some say Romulus himself struck him, others Celer, one of his companions; he fell, however, and in the scuffle Faustulus also was slain, and Plistinus, who, being Faustulus's brother, story tells us, helped to bring up Romulus.
(X, 1–2 [Dryden et al.])

Plutarch, *Roman and Greek Questions*

Why do they [i.e., the Romans] consider all fortifications sacred and inviolable but not gates? Or, as Varro wrote, must we consider a fortification sacred because people bravely fight and die upon it? Thus does it seem that Romulus, too, slew his brother because he tried to cross a sacred, inviolable site.

(270 F–271 A [S. S.])

Florus, *The Epitome of Roman History*

8. It was thought that a rampart was enough for the protection of the new city. In derision of its small size Remus leaped over it and was put to death for doing so, whether by his brother's order or not is uncertain; at any rate he was the first victim and hallowed the fortification of the new city with his blood.

(I, 1, 8. Translation by E. S. Forester, from Florus, *The Epitome of Roman History*, Loeb Classical Library [Cambridge, MA: Harvard University Press, 1929], http://penelope.uchicago.edu/Thayer/E/Roman/Texts/Florus/Epitome/1A*.html#I.)

Dionysius of Halicarnassus, *The Roman Antiquities*

30, 1. The other deeds reported of this man, both in his wars and at home, which may be thought deserving of mention in a history are as follows. 2. Inasmuch as many nations that were both numerous and brave in war dwelt round about Rome and none of them was friendly to the Romans, he desired to conciliate them by intermarriages, which, in the opinion of the ancients, was the surest method of cementing friendships; but considering that the cities in question would not of their own accord unite with the Romans, who were just getting settled together in one city, and who neither were powerful by reason of their wealth nor had performed any brilliant exploit, but that they would yield to force if no insolence accompanied such compulsion, he determined, with the approval of Numitor, his grandfather, to bring about the desired intermarriages by a wholesale seizure of virgins.

(II, 30, 1–2 [E. C.])

Livy, *The History of Rome*

1. The Roman State had now become so strong that it was a match for any of its neighbours in war, but its greatness threatened to last for only one generation, since through the absence of women there was no hope of offspring, and there was no right of intermarriage with their neighbours. 2. Acting on the advice of the senate, Romulus sent envoys amongst the surrounding nations to ask for alliance and the right of intermarriage on behalf of his new community. 3. It was represented that cities, like everything else, sprung from the humblest beginnings, and those who were helped on by their own courage and the favour of heaven won for themselves great power and great renown. 4. As to the origin of Rome, it was well known that whilst it had received divine assistance, courage and self-reliance were not wanting. There should, therefore, be no reluctance for men to mingle their blood with their fellow-men. 5. Nowhere did the envoys meet with a favourable reception. Whilst their pro-

posals were treated with contumely, there was at the same time a general feeling of alarm at the power so rapidly growing in their midst. Usually they were dismissed with the question, "whether they had opened an asylum for women, for nothing short of that would secure for them intermarriage on equal terms." 6. The Roman youth could ill brook such insults, and matters began to look like an appeal to force.

(I, 9, 1–6 [R.C.R.])

John Malalas, *Chronography*

Under the rule of this same Romus [*sic*], the army, made up of men from every provenance, grew a great deal in size, and Rome filled with a mob of rustic men, as there were no women among this number. The armies of youths felt a natural desire, and thus assailed the women in the square. Confusion broke out, and there was a row amongst the citizens. Knowing not what to do, Romus was discouraged, because none of the women consented to join with such rustic, barbarian soldiers. Thus he proclaimed a law according to which the soldiers would take virgins, which he called Brutids, in marriage, but no one would give his daughter. They said that because of the wars, those men would have no chance of so much as a normal life, and thus they gave their daughters to men of the city. Discouraged, Romus went to consult the oracle, and he received the reply that he should celebrate an equestrian spectacle for the women, so that the army could procure women for themselves.

(1, VII. CSHB, pp. 177–178 [S. S.])

Pompeii, *Eumachia Building*

Romulus son
of Mars built the city
of Rome and reigned
for forty-two years
As first leader
he killed the enemies' leader Acron,
king of the Caeninenses,
and offered to Jupiter Feretrius
his honorable spoils (*spolia opima*).
(CIL X 809 [S. S.])

Livy, *The History of Rome*

1. The feelings of the abducted maidens were now pretty completely appeased, but not so those of their parents. They went about in mourning garb, and tried by their tearful complaints to rouse their countrymen to action. Nor did they confine their remonstrances to their own cities; they flocked from all sides to Titus Tatius, the king of the Sabines, and sent formal deputations to him, for his was the most influential name in those parts. 2. The people of Caenina, Crustumerium, and Antemnae were the greatest sufferers; they thought Tatius and his Sabines were too slow in moving, so these three cities prepared to make war conjointly. 3. Such, however, were the impatience and anger of the Caeninensians that even the Crustuminians and Antemnates did not display enough energy for them, so the men of Caenina made an attack upon Roman territory

on their own account. 4. Whilst they were scattered far and wide, pillaging and destroying, Romulus came upon them with an army, and after a brief encounter taught them that anger is futile without strength. He put them to a hasty flight, and following them up, killed their king and despoiled his body; then after slaying their leader took their city at the first assault. 5. He was no less anxious to display his achievements than he had been great in performing them, so, after leading his victorious army home, he mounted to the Capitol with the spoils of his dead foe borne before him on a frame constructed for the purpose. He hung them there on an oak, which the shepherds looked upon as a sacred tree, and at the same time marked out the site for the temple of Jupiter, and addressing the god by a new title, uttered the following invocation: 6. "Jupiter Feretrius! these arms taken from a king, I, Romulus a king and conqueror, bring to thee, and on this domain, whose bounds I have in will and purpose traced, I dedicate a temple to receive the 'spolia opima' which posterity following my example shall bear hither, taken from the kings and generals of our foes slain in battle." 7. Such was the origin of the first temple dedicated in Rome. And the gods decreed that though its founder did not utter idle words in declaring that posterity would thither bear their spoils, still the splendour of that offering should not be dimmed by the number of those who have rivalled his achievement. For after so many years have elapsed and so many wars been waged, only twice have the "spolia opima" been offered. So seldom has Fortune granted that glory to men.

(I, 10, 1–7 [R.C.R.])

Propertius

Now I'll begin to reveal the origins of Feretrian Jupiter and the triple trophies won from three chieftains. I climb a steep path, but the glory of it gives me strength: I never delight in wreaths plucked on easy slopes.

Romulus, you set the pattern first for this prize, and returned burdened with enemy spoils, victorious at the time when Caeninian Acron was attempting the gates of Rome, whom you spilled with your spear from his fallen mount. Acron the chieftain from Caenina's citadel, descendant of Hercules, was once the scourge of your country, Rome. He dared to hope for spoils from Quirinus's shoulders, but gave his own, not un-moistened by his blood. Romulus saw him, testing his spear against the hollow towers, and anticipated him with a pre-destined vow: "Jupiter this Acron falls as a victim today to you." He vowed it and Acron fell as Jupiter's spoil.

(IV, 10, 1–16. Translation by A. S. Kline, © 2002, 2008, http://www.poetryintranslation.com/PITBR/Latin/PropertiusBkFour.htm.)

Plutarch, *Romulus*

1. The Sabines were a numerous and martial people, but lived in small, unfortified villages, as it befitted, they thought, a colony of the Lacedaemonians to be bold and fearless; nevertheless, seeing themselves bound by such hostages to their good behaviour, and being solicitous for their daughters, they sent ambassadors to Romulus with fair and equitable requests, that he would return their

young women and recall that act of violence, and afterwards, by persuasion and lawful means, seek friendly correspondence between both nations. 2.Romulus would not part with the young women, yet proposed to the Sabines to enter into an alliance with them; upon which point some consulted and demurred long, but Acron, king of the Ceninenses, a man of high spirit and a good warrior, who had all along a jealousy of Romulus's bold attempts, and considering particularly, from this exploit upon the women, that he was growing formidable to all people, and indeed insufferable, were he not chastised, first rose up in arms, and with a powerful army advanced against him. Romulus likewise prepared to receive him; 3. but when they came within sight and viewed each other, they made a challenge to fight a single duel, the armies standing by under arms, without participation. And Romulus, making a vow to Jupiter, if he should conquer, to carry himself, and dedicate his adversary's armour to his honour, overcame him in combat, and a battle ensuing, routed his army also, and then took his city; but did those he found in it no injury, only commanded them to demolish the place and attend him to Rome, there to be admitted to all the privileges of citizens. And indeed there was nothing did more advance the greatness of Rome, than that she did always unite and incorporate those whom she conquered into herself. 4. Romulus, that he might perform his vow in the most acceptable manner to Jupiter, and withal make the pomp of it delightful to the eye of the city, cut down a tall oak which he saw growing in the camp, which he trimmed to the shape of a trophy, and fastened on it Acron's whole suit of armour disposed in proper form; then he himself, girding his clothes about him, and crowning his head with a laurel garland, his hair gracefully flowing, 5. carried the trophy resting erect upon his right shoulder, and so marched on, singing songs of triumph, and his whole army following after, the citizens all receiving him with acclamations of joy and wonder. The procession of this day was the origin and model of all after triumphs. This trophy was styled an offering to Jupiter Feretrius, 6. from ferire, which in Latin is to smite; for Romulus prayed he might smite and overthrow his enemy; and the spoils were called opima, or royal spoils, says Varro, from their richness, which the word opes signifies; though one would more probably conjecture from opus, an act; for it is only to the general of an army who with his own hand kills his enemies' general that this honour is granted of offering the opima spolia. 7. And three only of the Roman captains have had it conferred on them: first, Romulus, upon killing Acron the Ceninensian; next, Cornelius Cossus, for slaying Tolumnius the Tuscan; and lastly, Claudius Marcellus, upon his conquering Viridomarus, king of the Gauls. The two latter, Cossus and Marcellus, made their entries in triumphant chariots, bearing their trophies themselves; but that Romulus made use of a chariot, Dionysius is wrong in asserting. 8. History says, Tarquinius, Damaratus's son, was the first that brought triumphs to this great pomp and grandeur; others, that Publicola was the first that rode in triumph. The statues of Romulus in triumph are, as may be seen in Rome, all on foot.

(XVI, 1–8 [Dryden et al.])

Cicero, *The Commonwealth*

This cause having brought on Rome the Sabine armies, and the issue of the battle being doubtful and undecided, Romulus made an alliance with Tatius, king of the Sabines, at the intercession of the matrons who had been so abducted. By this compact, he admitted the Sabines into the city, communicated with their religious ceremonies, and divided his power with their king.

(II, 13 [F. B.])

Dionysius of Halicarnassus, *The Roman Antiquities*

46, 1. . . . And first a truce was agreed upon between the two nations; then the kings met together and a treaty of friendship was concluded. 2. The terms agreed upon by the two, which they confirmed by their oaths, were as follows: that Romulus and Tatius should be kings of the Romans with equal authority and should enjoy equal honours; that the city, preserving its name, should from its founder be called Rome; that each individual citizen should as before be called a Roman, but that the people collectively should be comprehended under one general appellation and from the city of Tatius be called Quirites, and that all the Sabines who wished might live in Rome, joining in common rites with the Romans and being assigned to tribes and curiae. 3. After they had sworn to this treaty and, to confirm their oaths, had erected altars near the middle of the Sacred Way, as it is called, they mingled together. And all the commanders returned home with their forces except Tatius, the king, and three persons of the most illustrious families, who remained at Rome and received those honours which their posterity after them enjoyed; these were Volusus Valerius and Tallus, surnamed Tyrannius, with Mettius Curtius, the man who swam cross the lake with his arms, and with them there remained also their companions, relations and clients, no fewer in number than the former inhabitants.

(II, 46, 1–3 [E. C.])

Livy, *The History of Rome*

5. The last of these wars was commenced by the Sabines and proved the most serious of all, for nothing was done in passion or impatience; they masked their designs till war had actually commenced. 6. Strategy was aided by craft and deceit, as the following incident shows. Spurius Tarpeius was in command of the Roman citadel. Whilst his daughter had gone outside the fortifications to fetch water for some religious ceremonies, Tatius bribed her to admit his troops within the citadel. 7. Once admitted, they crushed her to death beneath their shields, either that the citadel might appear to have been taken by assault, or that her example might be left as a warning that no faith should be kept with traitors. 8. A further story runs that the Sabines were in the habit of wearing heavy gold armlets on their left arms and richly jewelled rings, and that the girl made them promise to give her "what they had on their left arms," accordingly they piled their shields upon her instead of golden gifts.

(I, 11, 5–8 [R.C.R.])

Livy, *The History of Rome*

2. Then it was that the Sabine women, whose wrongs had led to the war, throwing off all womanish fears in their distress, went boldly

into the midst of the flying missiles with dishevelled hair and rent garments. Running across the space between the two armies they tried to stop any further fighting and calm the excited passions by appealing to their fathers in the one army and their husbands in the other not to bring upon themselves a curse by staining their hands with the blood of a father-in-law or a son-in-law, nor upon their posterity the taint of parricide. 3. "If," they cried, "you are weary of these ties of kindred, these marriage-bonds, then turn your anger upon us; it is we who are the cause of the war, it is we who have wounded and slain our husbands and fathers. Better for us to perish rather than live without one or the other of you, as widows or as orphans." 4. The armies and their leaders were alike moved by this appeal. There was a sudden hush and silence. Then the generals advanced to arrange the terms of a treaty. It was not only peace that was made, the two nations were united into one State, the royal power was shared between them, and the seat of government for both nations was Rome. 5. After thus doubling the City, a concession was made to the Sabines in the new appellation of Quirites, from their old capital of Cures.

(I, 13, 2–5 [R.C.R.])

Valerius Maximus

During the reign of Romulus, Spurius Tarpeius was commander of the citadel [arx]. Tatius persuaded the latter's daughter, a virgin who had gone outside the walls to draw water for rites, to welcome the armed Sabines with her inside the citadel, after offering what they bore in their left hands as recompense: gold bracelets and rings of great weight. Taking possession of the site, the Sabine army then killed the girl when she asked for her reward, burying her under their weapons [i.e., their shields], thus keeping their promise, since they bore these, too, in their left hands. But let there be no reproach, as the treachery was avenged with swift punishment.

(IX, 6, 1 [S. S.])

Plutarch, *Romulus*

2. . . . . The rest of the Sabines, enraged hereat, choosing Tatius their captain, marched straight against Rome. The city was almost inaccessible, having for its fortress that which is now the Capitol, where a strong guard was placed, and Tarpeius their captain; not Tarpeia the virgin, as some say who would make Romulus a fool. But Tarpeia, daughter to the captain, coveting the golden bracelets she saw them wear, betrayed the fort into the Sabines' hands, and asked, in reward of her treachery, the things they wore on their left arms. 3. Tatius conditioning thus with her, in the night she opened one of the gates, and received the Sabines. And truly Antigonus, it would seem, was not solitary in saying he loved betrayers, but hated those who had betrayed; nor Caesar, who told Rhymitalces the Thracian, that he loved the treason, but hated the traitor; but it is the general feeling of all who have occasion for wicked men's service, as people have for the poison of venomous beasts; they are glad of them while they are of use, and abhor their baseness when it is over. 4. And so then did Tatius behave towards Tarpeia, for he commanded the Sabines, in regard to their contract, not to refuse

her the least part of what they wore on their left arms; and he himself first took his bracelet off his arm, and threw that, together with his buckler, at her; and all the rest following, she, being borne down and quite buried with the multitude of gold and their shields, died under the weight and pressure of them; 5. Tarpeius also himself, being prosecuted by Romulus, was found guilty of treason, as Juba says Sulpicius Galba relates.

(XVII, 2–5 [Dryden et al.])

Appian of Alexandria, *Excerpta de legationibus gentium*

When Tatius waged war against Romulus, the wives of the Romans, who were daughters of the Sabines, made peace between them. Advancing to the camp of the parents they held out their hands to them and showed the infant children already born to them and their husbands, and testified that their husbands had done them no wrong. They prayed that the Sabines would take pity on themselves, their sons-in-law, their grandchildren, and their daughters, and either put an end to this wretched war between relatives, or first kill them in whose behalf it was begun. The parents, moved partly by their own difficulties and partly by pity for the women, and perceiving that what the Romans had done was not from lust but necessity, entered into negotiations with them.

For this purpose Romulus and Tatius met in the street which was named from this event Via Sacra and agreed upon these conditions: that both Romulus and Tatius should be kings, and that the Sabines who were then serving in the army under Tatius, and any others who might choose to come, should be allowed to settle in Rome on the same terms and under the same laws as the Romans themselves.

(I, 5, 1. Translation by Horace White, from Appian, *Roman History* [New York: Bohn's Classical Library, 1899], http://www.livius.org/ap-ark/ appian/appian_kings.html.)

Index

Note: Page numbers in italic type indicate illustrations.